FOUNDATIONS OF MODERN HISTORY

General Editor A. Goodwin

Professor of Modern History, The University of Manchester

FOUNDATIONS OF MODERN HISTORY

Britain and Europe
in the Seventeenth Century

by J. R. JONES

Professor of English History in
the School of English Studies
The University of East Anglia

W · W · NORTON & COMPANY · INC ·
NEW YORK

General Preface

THIS series of short historical studies has as its main theme successive phases in the evolution of modern history from Renaissance times to the present day. Its general purpose is to provide within a limited compass, and at a reasonable cost, scholarly surveys of some of the fundamental developments which have influenced the civilization and conditioned the outlook of the modern world. A second aim of the series will be to illustrate how not only the general direction of recent historical inquiry but also its very content and its relatons with other disciplines have been progressively modified. If students of scientific or technological subjects who are extending their interests to the 'liberal' arts or social sciences are made aware of these trends something will have been done to close the gap between the scientific and humane cultures. A further feature of the series will be the endeavour to present selected periods of British history against the contemporary background of European development, with special emphasis on the nature and extent of cultural, scientific or intellectual interchange. Here the object will be to demonstrate the unity as well as the diversity of the European heritage and to re-examine its evolving significance in the context of global history.

In this volume, for example, Dr. Jones explains the ways in which, in the first half of the seventeenth century, British attitudes and domestic and foreign policies were deeply affected by European influences – political, economic and above all religious – and how, increasingly, as the century progressed, this position was reversed. If the mutual interaction of Britain and Western Europe is considered in this light our views of the historical significance of the English revolution of the 1640s will, as the author suggests, necessarily diverge from that of the nineteenth-century Whig historians and from the more recent interpretations of British and Continental Marxist historians. Both Whig and Marxist historians have tended to regard the 'conservative' revolution of 1688 as a mere appendage to the radical revolution of the middle years of the century. Considered in relation to Britain's final emergence as a great power and her impact on European and world affairs, the revolution of 1688 must, however, be regarded as the decisive turning point in British seventeenth-century development. This process was, as the author shows, a gradual one and his study is of great value in revealing, for example, not only the importance of British commercial interests in the Mediterranean even in the early years of Anglo-Dutch rivalry, but also the crucial significance of the period 1667–89 in the determination of Britain's subsequent role in Continental affairs.

Among other incidental points of re-interpretation which this analysis suggests may be mentioned the more understanding view of James I's pro-Spanish policy, the reassessment of Cromwell's achievements in foreign and colonial policy, the relative insignificance at this period of colonial conflicts between Britain and her Continental rivals, until at least the time of Colbert, the reality of the threats to British commerce represented by the French *guerres de course* under Louis XIV (which British naval historians have consistently underrated), the deep repercussions on English public opinion of the Revocation of the Edict of Nantes and the profound effects of the Nine Years war upon the British administrative and financial system.

The essential task of Dr. Jones, however, is to provide an explanation of British official and sectional reactions to the commercial ascendancy of the United Provinces in the first half of the seventeenth century and to the rise of the absolutist system of Louis XIV. His account of the Anglo-Dutch and Anglo-French wars in the context of the Counter-Reformation provides a more detailed and diversified treatment than is to be found in the more general histories and his scholarly evaluation of Dutch and French influence upon the British cultural tradition and material civilization at this period is not the least valuable aspect of his work of synthesis and re-interpretation.

Contents

CHAPTER ONE

Introduction

ALTHOUGH the seventeenth century has probably received more attention than any other period in British history, it can be said that a great many historians who have studied the period and written about it have shown a marked insularity in their approach to its developments and problems. The main thesis of this study is to emphasize the close interdependence of Britain and Europe in the seventeenth century, to show that events at home cannot be fully understood unless they are related to developments and forces abroad. Indeed in cultural and intellectual, as well as political and economic, matters, the effect on Britain of foreign influences is for most of this period greater than that of Britain on Europe; one of the main questions to be considered is why this relation was later reversed.

Writing in the 1960s, when the relationship between Britain and Western Europe has been, and is likely to become again, a matter of acute and general controversy, it would be easy to read back into the past our own partisan views and current preoccupations. This temptation must be resisted; we have before us the example of the classic Whig historians. For Hallam and Macaulay, and for Trevelyan and Churchill later, the period contained the decisive conflict between the cause of constitutional and religious liberty, which prevailed only in Britain, and the reactionary systems of absolutism, which generally triumphed throughout Europe. Their insular confidence, and their trust in the inevitable victory of the 'progressive' cause, coloured their view of the past. They condemned Stuart conduct of foreign affairs as severely as their domestic policy, drew an unfavourable comparison of a cowardly James I with the glorious Elizabeth, and regarded the profligate Charles II and his bigoted brother James as the puppets of Louis XIV. The Cromwellian interlude, if tyrannical at home, was depicted as glorious abroad, but only

William III received unreserved praise for both his home and his foreign policies. Only after 1688 were events abroad seen to have had a positive connection with developments at home; until then, apart from the sinister intervention of foreign powers – Spain in the reigns of James I and Charles I, France from 1660 to 1688 – events in Britain were presented as if they had taken place in a separate hemisphere.

William III, the hero of the Whigs, has been less favourably treated by more modern historians, including those who use Marxist analyses. For Marxists the 'Glorious Revolution' of 1688 was merely the final stage in the bourgeois capture of power, a postcript to, or consolidation of, the far more significant English Revolution of the 1640s and 1650s. Unlike the Whigs, they are concerned to relate developments in Britain to those in Europe. The English Revolution is interpreted as part of a 'general crisis' caused by the transition from feudal to bourgeois economic, social and ultimately political systems; it is compared with the mid-century movements and revolutions in France, Naples, Catalonia and even the Ukraine, but, surprisingly, far less attention has been paid to the political and social comparison with the Netherlands.

It is hoped that the generalizations which are inevitable in a study of restricted length will not be taken as facile simplifications, but will serve to provoke discussion, or will enable the reader to look at familiar topics from a new angle. I have tried to outline the basic position in cases where the subject is comparatively unexplored or wherever it is a matter of controversy, to suggest what questions have to be asked, and to indicate some of the reasons when, and why, historians are not satisfied with the answers which have been given in the past. Many of the arguments which I have put forward are, consciously, hypotheses rather than firm conclusions. In order to leave the text free for their development and examination, the general factual background is summarized in the time chart (pp. 113–116) to which reference should be made.

The biggest of all generalizations is to use such concepts as 'Britain' and 'Europe'. The relevant meanings of the latter should become apparent in the course of the survey, but in introduction I will detail the various classes, sections and interests which came into contact with seventeenth-century Europe.

1. Those who were professionally concerned with foreign affairs constituted only a small group, unrepresentative even of the political nation.

Decisions in the field of foreign affairs, constitutionally a matter for the royal prerogative, were usually made by a small, inner group of the Privy Council. The choice, and number, of these advisers were determined by many factors. Sometimes it was the need for secrecy or deception, as in the negotiations for the Spanish marriage, or before the Dover treaty of 1670. At times faction or favouritism prevailed, as in Buckingham's years of misrule before 1628, or the purpose was to gain the support of various groups, as during the Cabal period, 1670–73. No fixed rule or conventions existed as to who should make decisions, or how business should be transacted. Often everything depended on the King personally, as when Charles II concluded a treaty with France in 1681 or when William III negotiated the partition treaties.

Day to day business and correspondence were managed by the secretaries of state. Up to 1612 Salisbury acted alone; after his death there was a gap of two years, but after 1614 two secretaries were employed. During the rest of the century certain conventions were established to regulate and define their duties. Generally, after 1660, the senior secretary handled relations with the 'south', that is the two great powers France and Spain, Italy and the Mediterranean, Portugal, etc; while the junior had as his sphere the 'north', the Netherlands, Germany, Scandinavia and the Baltic. But there continued to be a wide variety in the type of person who held the office, the ways in which he obtained the appointment and executed its duties, his importance as a figure in domestic politics and his attitude to the conduct of foreign affairs. There was no uniformity or system. Normally secretaries had served abroad as diplomats, but even this was not essential. Some secretaries were leading politicians, others little more than clerks. Some had humble origins, many were aristocratic magnates of the first rank. The King appointed some because of their specialized knowledge of the particular foreign problems of the day, others for the quite unrelated task of managing the Commons. This total lack of system, and the wide and sometimes haphazard variation in the importance and efficiency of the office, show that foreign affairs played a comparatively unimportant part in domestic politics, at least until 1688. After the Revolution William himself acted as virtual director of foreign policy, but with Britain committed to war in Europe the office subsequently increased in potential significance. Bolingbroke, after 1710, was the first secretary to use this office as a position from which to make a bid for supreme power.

2. Under the supervision of the secretaries there existed a number of diplomatic posts abroad – it is impossible to speak of a 'diplomatic service', although some systematic organization can be discovered after 1688. At first there was only one permanent ambassador, at Constantinople, and this was because he was paid by the Levant Company, and not by the King. But either ambassadors or envoys (the title held by a representative depended largely on his personal status) were maintained at the major Courts – at Paris, Madrid, The Hague and in the earlier part of the century at Venice, and in the later years Vienna. Smaller countries received residents, while merchants acted as consuls in important ports. The most important post was undoubtedly Paris, a fact which was reflected in the quality of representatives there, by the number who subsequently served as secretaries of state and by the competition for the appointment. However, Britain was probably represented most efficiently at the The Hague, by a whole series of men of very different views but great ability: Winwood, Carleton, Strickland, Downing and Temple. After 1688 the regular presence of William and later Marlborough reduced the importance of the post.

On occasion permanent representatives could be supplemented by ambassadors sent on special missions, to negotiate an alliance or mediate a peace. James I made particular use of them during the early stages of the Thirty Years War, with complete lack of success; their high rank and lavish expenditure did not compensate for their inexperience and ignorance. There was a vital difference between such special ambassadors (for instance, Doncaster and Kensington, appointed in 1619 and 1624 respectively) and ordinary diplomats. The latter found themselves out of the mainstream of English life and politics through long residence abroad. Slow and unreliable communications isolated them. The lack of any system of training, selection or promotion kept diplomats inevitably and continuously dependent on some patron at home. The eternal problem of obtaining pay and allowances, and the constant fear of being supplanted by personal or political enemies, increased this dependence. Changes in the balance of politics at home could ruin their careers overnight. Moreover, prolonged residence abroad brought the insidious danger of becoming more French or Spanish than English in outlook, in sympathies and, above all and particularly at Madrid, in religion.

Aspirants to a diplomatic career generally obtained a recommendation from a minister or friend to a diplomat, and lived as one of his household. By this means some experience of business and knowledge of languages could be obtained, even if for many such service afforded merely a cheap and convenient form of foreign travel.

3. Many diplomats subsequently sat in Parliament, but it is remarkable what restricted influence they exerted; Sir William Temple is the most glaring example, a great man respected throughout Europe but a complete nullity at Westminster. This suggests one reason why the effects at home of the growing popularity of foreign travel among the upper classes should not be exaggerated.* Before 1604, the French civil wars and Habsburg enmity restricted private travel, but by the 1620s even the Papal States and countries of the Inquisition were (with tact and caution) safe for the wealthy traveller. The main value of travel was to complete a man's general education; in France, where they could easily enter the Court, young Englishmen were attracted by the fashions, modes of life and academies of the nobility, even if their parents and tutors preferred the Huguenot towns of the Loire valley and Languedoc. In Italy the monuments of classical antiquity formed the

---

* It is even harder to estimate the effect on the public of the popular travel books of the time, whose authors, for instance Fynes Moryson and William Lithgow, vividly communicated to their readers their robust insularity and strong Protestantism.

main attraction, followed closely by the cosmopolitan society to be found particularly in Venice and Padua. Renaissance art made a great appeal, although purchases were often by wealthy tourists for prestige purposes and without discrimination – so that many were foisted off with frauds.

No generalizations can be made on the impressions brought home by upper-class travellers, but one aspect of their experiences must have been of crucial importance. The main travel routes ran through predominantly Catholic countries. Most travellers, apart from recusants and secret sympathizers, must have set out with the prevalent national hostility to popery. When they saw Catholicism openly, and magnificently, practised what were their reactions? Many seem to have had their prejudices confirmed, but a few in each generation changed their faith, and by doing so cut themselves off from the majority of their fellow-countrymen; in fact many of these converts settled permanently abroad. After 1660, travellers faced a second test, in the impact made upon them by the new overwhelming greatness and power of France, which was symbolized by the permanent pageant of Louis XIV's court, and by the spectacular and obvious expansion of his army and navy. All were impressed, but most appreciated and feared the implications of this system of absolutism for their own country. Only among some of the lesser nobility, especially the Scots and Irish, does one find admiration and a desire to imitate the French.

The increasing popularity of foreign travel does not seem to have led to any broadening of views in Parliament before the civil war.* A majority of M.P.s in the 1620s belonged to the older generation which had had less opportunity for foreign travel. The royalists in the Long Parliament were significantly younger than the parliamentarians, and seem to have been far more widely travelled, but they lost control over policy with the outbreak of the civil war, although knowledge of foreign countries was to help those who went into exile during the interregnum. Among the parliamentarians there was one group with a special kind of foreign experience, those who had served

---

* Foreign experience is an aspect of members' lives which has been quite unjustifiably ignored by the compilers of collective parliamentary biographies.

abroad as soldiers, mainly in the Dutch army. These men, together with those who had served in Ireland, formed the most articulate and vehement group expressing 'Protestant' views on foreign affairs. Private soldiers were sometimes pressed for service, as for Mansfeld's army in 1624, or driven abroad by economic conditions, but a high proportion of both officers and men fought for a definite cause as well as for a livelihood. Those who returned. brought back with them a simple but coherent view of European affairs, and they were to play a vital part in the civil wars. The Dutch service was also one of the earliest dumping grounds for poor relations, the younger sons of the aristocracy and gentry, and for undesirables generally. Many of the adventurers returned to serve the King, and there was also an influx from the Spanish service which attracted Catholics, partly to serve the King but also to fight for the Irish Confederates.

4. Apart from those who went into exile during the interregnum, comparatively few of the Anglican clergy travelled abroad – a very significant fact. Those who did usually acted as chaplains to small, almost besieged English communities, or went as tutors to young men making the Grand Tour, a difficult task in which they had to protect their charges from the temptations of vice and the proselytizing of Catholic priests. Very few attended continental universities. Individuals corresponded with foreign scholars of other confessions, as George Bull did with Bossuet, but such contact was intermittent until the latitudinarians began to contribute to the regular intellectual communication of the 'republic of letters' towards the end of the century. Most clergy remained comparatively uninterested in foreign churches; for them Protestantism meant the Reformed, that is Calvinist, churches, and few had any real knowledge of Lutheranism until the years just before the Hanoverian succession.

In the case of English Puritanism, insularity was a development of the seventeenth century. During Elizabeth's reign, when its strongholds were at the universities, Puritan scholars had constantly corresponded with foreign Calvinists, travelled and often lived and ministered abroad. This tradition weakened. Men like William Ames who taught at a Dutch university, published in Latin and attended the synod of Dort, were replaced by a generation who placed greater emphasis on pastoral work and published in English. English Puritanism and Nonconformity became increasingly self-centred; New England and, after 1688, Scotland, constituted its external influences, although all contact with Dutch and French Calvinists was never lost. It was not until the early years of the eighteenth century that Dutch Arminianism and rational theology began to work among English Nonconformists.

5. The insularity of the Anglican clergy was a source of strength at the time; the Catholics suffered because of their cosmopolitanism. Their clergy owed allegiance to a foreign sovereign, the Pope; they received their education at seminaries abroad and were often protected by foreign ambassadors in London. Most sons of upper-class recusant families went abroad for education and a high proportion, especially of younger sons, never returned permanently – they remained to train for the priesthood, entered regiments in Spanish or French service or served as factors for English merchants. Daughters frequently entered religious orders, which expanded during the century to keep pace with the demand. Travellers met such Catholic exiles, lay or clerical, all over Europe, but most of them became absorbed into the local population within two generations. Only where exiles congregated in large numbers could they retain their national identity. Such concentrations naturally alarmed the English and Irish governments since they were to be found in those strategic territories just across the sea which, first under Spain and then under France, posed a threat to British security. This association of exiles with the state, which besides claiming to be the champion of Catholicism happened also to be the main threat to the balance of power in Europe, is one reason for the continued hostility shown to what may seem to us to have been a small and harmless minority. The other chief reason was the disturbing contrast between the survival of a Catholic minority here (a majority in Ireland) and the rapid extermination of Protestantism in Bohemia, France and Hungary, which filled Englishmen with fear as well as hatred.

6. Merchants. The dependence of the economy on foreign

trade, and the consequent importance of the merchant classes, should need no emphasis. But the word 'merchant' was used to describe many different types of traders, from prosperous retailers to great London capitalists, and there never at any time existed a unified 'mercantile' or 'bourgeois' interest as distinct from (or even opposed to) the landed interest. Merchants were divided by function and occupation; exporters and importers, members and non-members of joint-stock or regulated companies, London merchants and those belonging to the out-ports, shippers and shipowners. In addition the merchant class as a whole, and most if not all of its sections, were divided into competing and hostile groups, factions and interests by a variety of factors – economic, social, personal and political. We still do not know enough about the basis for these groupings, their relation one to another, their respective attitudes to political, economic and social questions and issues, or their actual connections with the politics of Court, Parliament, City and country. A central question relates to the connection between business groups and the government. Some were attached to Stuart policy both before 1640 and after 1660 by the receipt of privileges, or by coincident self-interest, but this does not mean that they could, as a result, control or even influence its direction. The relation of merchant interests to interregnum governments, especially the Long Parliament and the Rump, needs clarification. Even in the apparently straightforward subject of hostility to the Dutch, the part played by economic motives needs to be carefully related to the influence exerted by political, ideological and diplomatic forces. It must be stressed that England (and still more Scotland, Ireland and Wales) were basically agricultural countries, and that the landed classes possessed decisive influence in politics and economics. Nevertheless ministers and M.P.s, as well as merchants, recognized that increased wealth depended on the expansion of foreign trade. As in other countries 'mercantilist' policies, aimed at stimulating industry, exports, shipping and fisheries, were advocated and attempted. How far these efforts actually contributed to economic advance and expansion, or how far they served to enrich sectional interests at the expense of the nation as a whole, were questions acrimoniously debated throughout the century.

7. Seafarers. The Europe which merchants and seamen knew was a very different one from that of the Grand Tour. Few gentlemen travelled to North and Eastern Europe, but the important Baltic trades in corn, hides and especially naval stores employed a great many seamen and created merchant communities in Riga, Elbing and Danzig. Our closest cultural links were with France, but in commerce Holland, Zeeland and Hamburg were more important. In Italy, Rome and Venice outshone all other tourist attractions; the new free-port of Leghorn (Livorno) became the centre for our trade. Spain was off the map for all but hardy or eccentric travellers, but each port from Bilbao to Barcelona contained small merchant communities. There, even more than in the Baltic countries and the Levant, they lived in tightly knit and self-contained communities, insulated from the life, customs and religion of those who surrounded them.

Seamen could not help becoming perpetually embroiled in trouble, and their experiences in the raw, brutal and dangerous life at sea and ashore, in peace and in war, went far to create the popular image of Europe and the outside world. It may be objected that this is unimportant since seamen, and the working class of which they formed a part, could not directly influence governmental or mercantile policy. They did, however, play a (perhaps *the*) decisive role in the civil war, when the fleet spontaneously adhered to Parliament, and their part in forming the general climate of opinion was very considerable – faint echoes can still be heard in shanties and folk-lore. Three main points may be emphasized. First, seafaring was not always a lifelong occupation; a steady turnover of labour meant that there were perhaps ten times as many men with maritime experience living ashore as the 30,000 or so sailors employed at sea. Moreover, every large town (even York and Norwich) was a port. Secondly, the impact of war on seafarers was unbelievably heavier than on any other part of the population. Prices might be affected, the cloth trade suffer disruption, taxes increase, but war did not affect anyone so harshly as it did the seaman. He was pressed for the King's service; this was at any time cruelly hard and dangerous, but never did seamen suffer so much as in the second Dutch war when survivors of the bloody sea-battles were often discharged without pay to die of starvation or, with their trapped families, of plague. If a seaman remained in a merchantman he risked death or capture as soon as he put out to sea. No calculation can be made of the total damage suffered from the operations of enemy privateers during the Dutch and French wars; naval historians have consistently played down the significance of the *guerre de course* (on the ground that it could not be decisive), but its effects on the seafaring population were catastrophic. The war of 1625–30 against Spain does not feature prominently in textbooks, which mention only the attack on Cadiz, but for thousands of seamen it meant death or miserable captivity at Dunkirk, and the damage inflicted by privateers helped to plunge the country into a major economic depression. Dunkirk, first under Spain and then under France, became throughout the century a synonym for losses, capture, cruelty and death, and there were many other privateering bases almost as dangerous – Flushing, St. Malo, Lorient, Santander and Algiers. Thirdly, almost all seamen were fiercely anti-Catholic. Puritan, and later Nonconformist, ideas made a strong appeal to the more sober, but one may suspect that for many seamen anti-Catholicism was in itself a negative substitute for religion. A great deal of trade was with ports of Catholic Europe, and both resident merchants and visiting seamen could hardly avoid becoming involved in incidents, usually when relics or the sacrament were carried in procession through the streets. In countries where the Inquisition operated all Protestants were treated with extreme suspicion, and often mercilessly harried and savagely persecuted.

8. Aliens in Britain. More work is needed on the number and importance of immigrants, and on the attitude of contemporaries towards them. Catholic foreigners were found mainly in London, where they formed a community associated with the court, foreign embassies and native recusants. They were loathed because of their religion, the fact that most of them were French by origin and because they resisted assimilation. Attitudes towards Protestant foreigners were more ambivalent. Popular sympathies were aroused on behalf of the Huguenots in the 1620s and 1680s, but their Calvinism was distasteful to some of the Anglican hierarchy. In theory the government

knew that, as in the previous century, foreigners could strengthen the economy with capital, new trades and new techniques. The working class saw things differently. Often they regarded all foreigners with sharp hostility – for instance, the Palatine refugees in Anne's reign. Foreign employers were denounced for failing to employ native apprentices, new techniques were alleged to cause unemployment and foreign artisans were seen as competitors in the labour market. Serious riots did occur, significantly in times of depression, and gave the authorities reason to fear a repetition of the massacre of 'Ill May-day' of Henry VIII's time.

9. Ireland. As in other centuries Irish relations with Europe differed radically from those of England. All sections of the Catholic majority looked abroad – for education, for religious sustenance, for careers or for asylum. For the first half of the century Spain offered the best opportunities, and as the great Catholic power was regarded as the potential protector. Spanish territories sheltered seminaries and colleges, Spanish regiments attracted officers and soldiers, and there was some direct trade between the two countries. Later France replaced Spain in this role, and with the rise of the French navy and the construction of the naval base at Brest, there was an acute threat to British security even before the campaigns of 1689–91, which left such an impression on all subsequent Irish history.

10. Scotland. The relations of Lowland Scotland with Europe did not differ significantly from those of England but, as in most aspects of life, the Highlands were a separate case, more akin to the Irish pattern. Apart from some trade with France, and aristocratic links going back to the 'auld alliance', Scotland's main overseas connections were with the Netherlands. But, in sharp contrast to that of England, trade with Europe was generally stagnant until after the act of Union.

During the seventeenth century English commerce expanded into new trades and new areas, so that the country was bound to become more widely involved in European affairs even before it became involved in the actual diplomatic system as a principal. Trade protection required a naval presence in the Mediterranean from the 1650s, and we were also impelled to intervene in crises over the Sound in order to secure access to the Baltic. Of all connections the closest were with Spain, France and the Dutch; we were constantly involved with all three as allies or as enemies in the political as well as in the commercial and colonial fields. The main emphasis must, however, be placed on relations with France and the United Provinces. Spain was at first the great power in Europe. Her ambassadors intervened in English politics. However, culturally and ideologically her influence was slight, except on recusants. In France and the United Provinces, on the other hand, Englishmen could see societies, cultures, ideologies, institutions and economics all sufficiently alike our own to be comparable, and yet vitally different both from ours and from each other's. All educated Englishmen were attracted and repelled by various aspects of French and Dutch life; writers constantly advocated their conscious rejection or their emulation and imitation.

The final point to be made in introduction is to explain why the main emphasis must be placed on the latter part of the period. Until the decisive year, 1667, the choice between France and the United Provinces was implicit; thereafter it was explicit and unavoidable – although the final decision was not to be made until 1688.* In the perspective of relations with Europe the Revolution of the seventeenth century is that of 1688, not the 'English Revolution' of the mid-century. Only after 1688 did Britain become a European power of any consequence, but it must be emphasized that this was not an easy or an automatic process. The real revolution, it might be said, came in the painful and difficult process of readjustment which had to be made in every aspect of life during the wars against France. The wars against Spain and the Dutch may be described as trade wars; the wars against Louis XIV were for nothing less than national survival.

* For the importance of developments in 1667, see pages 73–5.

CHAPTER TWO

Britain and Europe, 1603–42

POPULAR historians have usually described the years 1603–42 as an inglorious period in comparison with the Elizabethan Age. Of course it must be said that James I was far less capable, yet much more ambitious, than Elizabeth, that his policies ended in humiliating and muddled failures, and that the last years of his reign were a time of prolonged economic depression. However, there are two qualifications to be made. First, too much emphasis should not be placed on diplomatic and political events; some branches of trade expanded, laying a basis for future economic developments of great importance, and there was a considerable growth of cultural and intellectual connections with Europe. Secondly, the basis of much seventeenth-century criticism of Stuart foreign policies, on which the Whig historians relied, was negative and unrealistic. It is a mark of the prejudiced and stubborn insularity of a majority of the popular and parliamentary critics that their case varied so little through the century, and that they should have learnt so little from experience. They enshrined Elizabeth in an entirely unhistorical myth of glory, and they took no account of the changes which were continually modifying Britain's relationships with Europe. They persisted in calling for a 'Protestant' foreign policy, in regarding all Catholic powers as hostile. The critics demanded exclusively maritime and colonial war, denouncing continental alliances and campaigns as unnecessary. Such an attitude may have been appropriate in the eighteenth-century wars against France, but historians have tended to overestimate the importance in the seventeenth century both of extra-European trade and of colonies as a cause of wars, and as strategic objectives in the conduct of wars.

However unsuccessful in their results, James's policies were at least an attempt at adjustment to the changes which were transforming Europe. He wisely concluded peace with Spain in 1604. The last stages of the war had not been very profitable; privateering (except apparently in the Mediterranean) had ceased to pay well, and the enemy had learnt to hit back through the dreaded Dunkirkers. The financial burden was increasing because of rapidly mounting prices and costs. National security had been assured by the defeat of Tyrone in Ireland. The peace itself conceded nothing that was vital: Spain did not obtain a total renunciation of trade with the Indies, but only of those parts it effectively occupied, the Catholics did not receive legal rights in religion, the cautionary towns in the Netherlands continued to be held by English garrisons. The peace brought material advantages. Royal finances gained temporary relief. Most valuable was the opening to traders of the Spanish possessions in Europe. Merchants were hampered by seizures of ships for trading with the Turks, and by protracted law cases over customs and smuggling, but it was trade in and with the Mediterranean which expanded fastest and most profitably during the first decades of the century. Solid gains from legal trade were more attractive than the lure of enormous, if hypothetical, profits to be made from the conquests in the New World which Raleigh advocated. Spanish merino wool was needed for the 'new draperies' which captured Mediterranean markets and offset the decline of the older types of textiles. A favourable balance of trade with Spain produced a regular inflow of bullion. The Spanish Netherlands offered a valuable market to which the Merchant Adventurers considered returning. Thus economic ties underlaid the *rapprochement* with Spain – as in the time of Henry VIII.

This fact was not appreciated by parliamentary critics, who belonged mainly to the landed classes. They believed that James's correct place was at the head of the European Protestant interest, united to defy all Catholic sovereigns. For the critics, advantages in trade did not outweigh their fears of Spanish power and ambition. They believed that Spain had both the military capability and the considered intention to strive for 'universal monarchy', and that its plans were being actively promoted by a 'Spanish party' at court – a charge which has been echoed by historians but is at present being subjected to critical examination. There is no doubt that the

Howard group at court, headed by Northampton, accepted
Spanish pensions and consisted largely of crypto-Catholics,
but this does not mean that they were traitors or acted as
mere instruments of Spanish policy. They were as convinced
by the advantages of peace as much as by Spanish money when
they resisted pressure for an aggressively 'Protestant' foreign
policy. The Howards used Spain for purposes of their own, and
in any case they never completely dominated James. For
instance they could not prevent him encouraging Venice to
defy Spanish pressure in 1619. The return that Spain got for
its money was a group at court and in the Council which acted
as a counterweight to the 'Protestant' and pro-French interests,
the latter consisting largely of Scottish nobles.

Obsessed as they were with Spanish power and ambition,
most Englishmen virtually ignored France – as had been
possible during the religious wars of the previous century –
and did not realize that under Henri IV she had re-emerged as
a great power whose interests and policies might clash with
ours. They would not admit that lack of resources compelled
Britain, if she was to follow an active European policy, to
choose between a French and a Spanish orientation. Instead
English opinion was concentrated almost entirely on the Huguenots, who were still regarded as the outer bulwark of our own
defences, comparable in importance to the Dutch, and as being
entitled in return to call on the King of England for protection.
Surprisingly, and in contrast to his suspicion of the Dutch as
rebels, James was ready to accept this role. He sent emissaries
to Huguenot assemblies, and repeatedly claimed the right to
mediate on their behalf with Louis XIII. All this was unrealistic, because of the abrupt decline in Huguenot political strength.
Some of their aristocratic adherents, like Rohan and Bouillon,
would use Britain (or Spain) for factious purposes of their own,
but the bourgeois appreciated the danger of appealing to a
weak England for protection against their own sovereign.

The prevalent English attitude towards the Dutch was
unrealistic and obsolescent for the opposite reasons. Englishmen saw them as our natural friends, almost dependents, tied
by 'the bond of love on our part towards those we have pre-
served from bondage and the like bond of their thankfulness
towards us'. After 1604 many followed events in the Nether-

lands with anxiety, wondering if the Dutch could stand alone. Only the comparatively few who were directly affected expressed sustained resentment at the outrageous Dutch attacks on our ships and traders in the Arctic and the East Indies. The nation as a whole was slow to realize that in both the military and economic fields the United Provinces were fast becoming a major power. Except in the Mediterranean it was the Dutch, not the English, who achieved an ascendancy in trade, and it was all the more frustrating that often the English pioneered new trades, like the Russian and the Greenland whale fisheries, only to be forcefully supplanted by the Dutch. Eventually hostility towards them was to build up, but during James's reign his own distaste for the Dutch, because it was based on his detestation of rebellion, was not shared by many of his subjects. They interpreted it as further evidence of his subservience to Spain, the 'Spanish party' and to Gondomar, the Spanish ambassador.

James's apparent infatuation with Spain, and the alleged ascendancy gained over him by Gondomar, were deeply resented by contemporaries and have been denounced by most historians. The assumptions which underlaid his persistent attempts to achieve an *entente* with Spain need therefore to be emphasized. First, Spain was the major European power so that without her co-operation general peace could not be obtained. Secondly, James cannot be blamed for believing in the early years of his reign that the long period of religious wars was coming to an end, and that consequently a permanent equilibrium could be established between Catholics and Protestants. James saw himself as a mediator and pacificator, in his more fanciful moments bringing together all confessions into one common faith; but at least he was trying to escape from the sterile position of regarding all Catholic states as axiomatic enemies. He had reconciled England and Scotland, and he later mediated successfully between Sweden and Denmark, Sweden and Russia, Venice and Savoy and Venice and Spain. But in trying to act as a universal mediator he went far beyond what was practicable. Lack of resources weakened his occasional threats, inconsistency affected his reputation, and

James and his servants simply lacked the skill, experience and knowledge of European affairs to be able materially to influence the course of events.

James intended that the marriage of his daughter Elizabeth to Frederick, Elector Palatine, in 1613, should be deliberately balanced by a Spanish marriage for Charles. James had not realized that Frederick's minister, Christian of Anhalt, had intended the Palatine marriage and a treaty which James signed with the Evangelical Union, of which Frederick was head, to commit England to a militantly Protestant policy in Germany. Similarly James seems to have had no insight into Spanish motives behind the protracted marriage negotiations. At first the Spaniards intended them primarily to block French approaches. Only when Gondomar arrived as ambassador in 1614 did the negotiations become serious. His ultimate aim was the conversion of Britain to Catholicism, to be achieved through either James or Charles embracing the faith; and this, in an age of *cuius regio eius religio*, was not so foolish as Victorian historians thought, with their belief in Britain's destiny as a Protestant country. Moreover, conversion of the sovereign, together with the marriage, would bring Britain permanently within the Spanish orbit. In the short term, the negotiations in themselves would ensure that a series of treaties which James had signed with Savoy, Denmark, the Dutch and some German princes would not become, as a few councillors hoped they would, an anti-Habsburg *bloc*.

The outbreak of the Thirty Years War, after Frederick had disregarded James's advice and usurped the Bohemian throne, multiplied his problems. At first, when they were weak, the Habsburgs accepted James's offers of mediation, only to disregard them after their victory at the White Mountain in 1620. English public opinion was apathetic at first, having little knowledge of, or interest in, the problems of Central Europe. A voluntary loan failed miserably, few volunteers came forward. But the attack on Frederick's own territories, by a Spanish army acting nominally under Imperial orders, created a crisis. A small English army under Vere tried to resist the Spaniards, the Dutch appealed for support. The reaction of the House of Commons was largely irrelevant. Members preferred to demand repression of recusants at home and a purely maritime war against Spain, to voting money for intervention on the Continent. Their vehement language, and in particular their attacks on the Spanish marriage negotiations were resented by James as encroachments on his prerogative. He chose to persist with the negotiations as the only way of obtaining the restoration of the Palatinate and stopping the spread of the war.

In fact, although promises of restoration were made, Spain was not in a position to fulfil them, because of the involvement of Imperial and Bavarian interests. Nevertheless, continuation of the marriage negotiations served a purpose from the Spanish point of view, by neutralizing Britain, even if, as the Spanish Council recognized in November 1622, they must ultimately fail. James characteristically and obstinately refused to admit this. From the start he was faced with demands from Spain that the Infanta should have the right to exercise her religion publicly, that her children should be educated as Catholics and that the penal laws should be repealed. These difficulties could hardly have been overcome, especially the last since it would require a parliamentary statute; but James never tried seriously to resolve them. He could not confess that the whole project had been futile from the beginning, and that there was no peaceful means of regaining the Palatinate. Towards the end, in 1622–24, he made one concession after another, as did Charles and Buckingham during their stay in Madrid. Even after their return, in October 1623, when they belatedly turned against the marriage and demanded war, James still tried to continue negotiations.

During the years 1622–28 Buckingham ruled Britain. The methods which he used in government, and in consolidating his position by the control of patronage, still need detailed investigation, but his whole career of self-aggrandizement and misrule illustrates the importance of purely personal considerations under the Stuart system of government. Personal favour, originating in a homosexual relationship with James, brought him supreme power. Apart from an attempt at reform and reconstruction of the navy he seems to have made no positive use of it. Beyond some experience of the French court, and a share of the essential political gift of using men cleverer than himself, Buckingham had no qualifications to conduct foreign affairs. He failed to overcome any of the difficulties which he encountered – diplomatic, parliamentary, adminstrative and military. His ambitious plans in 1624–25 for a grand alliance against Spain ignored European realities. Each power tried to exploit Britain for its own purposes. Sweden wanted more money than could be provided. Savoy hoped to use an English fleet against Genoa. The mercenary general Mansfeld saw in James a new source of income. Perhaps the most abject failure in all British military history resulted from the attempt to recover the Palatinate by providing him with an army. Several thousand wretches were illegally pressed, shipped abroad in colliers and died on board while the powers quarrelled over their employment. The Dutch wanted them for their own operations. France was more devious, aiming to involve Britain in a permanent conflict against Spain without committing herself – as might have happened if Mansfeld's men had been allowed to land at Calais. The marriage negotiations with France confirmed this fact; Louis XIII would not consider a full alliance between equals. He demanded ships from Britain to suppress Huguenot privateers, concessions for the recusants in the British Isles and full exercise of her religion for Henrietta Maria, but he offered only a dowry in return, and deliberately vague promises over the Palatinate.

The offensive against Spain in 1625 took the form of a naval expedition like that of 1596. The fleet, with soldiers embarked, was to capture shipping, seize and perhaps hold an Atlantic port (Lisbon, Cadiz or San Lucar), intercept the treasure fleet and attack the Spanish Indies. Even one of these tasks proved to be too difficult. The long delays in mounting the expedition revealed the limitations of English resources and the inadequacies of Buckingham's adminstration of the navy. Money was desperately short. Arms proved defective, the recruits needed more training and equipment than they could be given. Without the experienced officers, quartermasters and engineers who were seconded from the Dutch service the force could not even have started. There was not a single capable naval commander, the military officers quarrelled violently and soldiers and seamen died in overcrowded, insanitary ships. Troops were landed near Cadiz, but all opportunities were missed through lethargy or cowardice – only the allied Dutch contingent even tried to fight. After a few days the force had to be evacuated without achieving anything. The rest of the war, apart from Sir Kenelm Digby's spectacular raid on Spanish and neutral shipping in the Mediterranean, was occupied with ineffective attempts to protect merchant shipping from the constant attacks of the Dunkirkers. Losses appear to have been serious – over 300 ships – but their effect on the economy still needs evaluation.

Buckingham's provocation of a simultaneous war against France in 1627 can only be described as lunatic. After the negotiations for a Spanish marriage broke down he plunged into the treaty for a French match without realizing its one-sided nature. Subsequently the concessions made to the Catholics were repudiated in order to placate Parliament, the promise of ships for use against the Huguenots had to be broken when the seamen refused to serve. Richelieu made repeated and genuine attempts to avoid a break, but Buckingham deliberately aggravated the disputes, hoping that a war in defence of the Huguenots would be popular. In fact, only the aristocratic faction of Rohan and Soubise, who were already in rebellion, invited English intervention. When Buckingham sailed to the relief of La Rochelle the city had not broken with Louis XIII and had not asked for help. The citizens hesitated before taking the decisive step of making an agreement with him. So far from getting any material assistance, they actually supplied Buckingham's army during his campaign on the near-by Ile de Ré. The French drove this army off the island and repulsed two feeble relief expeditions in 1628, failures which were mainly due to defective preparations and supply. Maladministration, and an economic depression which was itself caused partly by the wars, prevented the government from mobilizing enough resources to mount a successful operation, still less a major campaign. These revelations of weakness contrasted with the power of the United Provinces, who for five years virtually sustained the anti-Habsburg cause. The parliamentary opposition was confirmed in its reluctance to support any but purely naval wars – the one success of the French war was Pennington's sweep of shipping in the Channel, and the sale of these prizes to finance the expeditions of La Rochelle was taken as proof that wars could be fought without heavy taxation. The officers who were seconded from the Dutch service reacted differently. Wimbledon blamed the failures on a decline of martial spirit among the upper classes and inexperience of war. Secondly, for the same reasons that he and other officers supported the Orangists in Dutch politics, he believed that the needs of security required a stronger executive. The King should be able to impose taxes whenever he judged them to be necessary for defence – an argument which was being used throughout Europe to justify royal absolutism.

During the years 1629–40 Charles could not afford an active foreign policy. He ended the French war in 1629, the Spanish in 1630, and for the rest of these years he and most of his ministers (including Wentworth and Laud) were absorbed by the problems of domestic, and especially financial, administration. Foreign affairs were left largely to Portland and Cottington who, as Lord Treasurer and Chancellor of the Exchequer, knew that financial stringency limited any possible action. They were often labelled pro-Spanish at the time, and other ministers as pro-French, but neither France nor Spain was greatly interested in Britain. She was neither valued as an ally nor feared as an enemy. Both countries engaged in desultory negotiations for an alliance, but they were satisfied if Britain was neutralized.

Nevertheless it would be wrong to describe the years of Personal Government as unimportant. They saw the beginning of policies and trends which, although restricted during this period and temporarily checked by the civil wars, were to come to fruition after the Restoration. Neutrality was seen to benefit trade. Reconstruction of the navy was undertaken in an attempt to assert sovereignty over the narrow seas. Finally, a wider outlook among a section of the upper classes gave Charles's court a cosmopolitan and cultured character including, fatally, a tolerant attitude towards Catholicism.

Economic recovery from the depression of 1630 was uneven. Some trades, notably the old draperies with their markets in Central and Eastern Europe disrupted by war and intensive Dutch competition, remained depressed. Significantly reinforcing the arguments of the so-called 'Spanish party', who stood for non-involvement in European wars rather than for intervention on the Habsburg side, the trades which flourished most were those connected with Spain. Merchants exploited Britain's neutral position so as to gain some advantages in relation to the Dutch. Only in the Mediterranean, where English ships were employed between Spanish-controlled ports, did they have an edge over the Dutch in the carrying trade. Military and commercial cargoes were shipped into Flemish ports in defiance of the Dutch blockade. Dover became an entrepôt for goods interchanged between Spain and Scandinavia and the Baltic – the very type of trade on which the prosperity of Amsterdam had been built. Imports from the East Indies were re-exported to Mediterranean countries. Bullion was shipped from Spain, coined at the Mint and then transported to the Spanish Netherlands, the King being paid a commission. Warships were used to convoy, and sometimes convey, contraband. Spanish troops were landed at Plymouth, taken overland to Dover and embarked for the short crossing to Dunkirk. Dunkirk privateers were allowed to shelter and refit in English and Scottish ports.

These activities in favour of Spain inevitably caused a steady deterioration in relations with the United Provinces. It is true that commercial rivalry with the Dutch, and their failure to give reparation for damages suffered in the East Indies, led many commercial interests to support royal policies, but opinion generally still sympathized with the Dutch as fellow-Protestants. Charles I's policies were personal rather than national, they were the work of a restricted group of courtiers, acting largely in their own interests, and those of groups of business and financial associates. This is a subject which requires more investigation, but the outlines seem to be clear. For instance, the East India Company had suffered most from the Dutch, and welcomed royal pressure on them, but its members were unnecessarily antagonized by royal approval of the establishment of a rival company by Courten. The Soap monopoly and the Fisheries' company actually impeded those who were already struggling in the face of Dutch competition. Similarly the construction of a formidable fleet did not bring direct benefits to the merchant community who helped to finance it through ship-money. The ostensible purposes of this fleet were to protect shipping from corsairs and privateers, and to enforce grandiose claims to the sovereignty of the 'British' seas. In practice it was used primarily as a means of raising revenue, like so many other aspects of the Personal Government. The fleet did not prove particularly effective in protecting commerce, instead it was employed in the attempt to exact money from Dutch fishing vessels in the North Sea. In 1639, when a Spanish fleet took refuge in the Downs, the sheltered anchorage within the Goodwins, Pennington was ordered to protect it with the English fleet, while Charles demanded £150,000 from Spain as the price of protection, and help towards the restoration of the Palatinate from France as the price of betrayal. Eventually Pennington was a virtually helpless spectator when Tromp attacked in what were, by any definition, British waters. Nevertheless the fleet was a potential challenge to Dutch power and prosperity; it would give teeth to English policy, whereas Charles's remarkably inconsistent intrigues during the 1630s possessed no practical importance. In 1631 and 1635 he actually agreed to a joint attack on the United Provinces, and their partition, in an alliance with Spain which was never ratified. This was hardly reconcilable with his clandestine negotiations in 1632 and 1633, behind Spain's back, for the establishment of a protectorate over the Spanish Netherlands, still less with negotiations in 1637 for an anti-Spanish alliance with the French and the Dutch.

Charles's friendship with Spain was popularly associated with the increased influence of Catholicism which was so obvious at court. By this time the special relationship between Spain and Catholicism was diminishing in intimacy, and Spanish cultural influences on thought, art and literature were far less than those of France, Italy and even the Spanish Netherlands. Sympathy towards Catholicism was a facet of the cosmopolitan, cultured and tolerant atmosphere of court circles; it was personal, based often on an artistic sympathy for its forms of worship, a product of extensive foreign travel or residence abroad. But this fashionable lack of prejudice against Catholicism could not help having political implications. The Queen was hated as the conscious instrument of the Pope and of Louis XIII in a campaign for the conversion of Britain. Henrietta Maria did in fact look on herself as a missionary, and in demonstrating her sympathies caused Charles worry and unpopularity. But, in contrast to the later situation under Charles

II and James II, Catholicism and absolutism were not in reality indissolubly linked. The 'Spanish party' consisted largely of death-bed Catholics who would not take personal risks for their religion. The Queen acted provocatively, but her practical importance was limited. Her connections were with the dissident elements in France – her brother Gaston, her exiled mother and Mme de Chevreuse – so that as long as Richelieu lived she could not expect official French support. She was, moreover, a woman of limited intelligence, with incompetent and disreputable advisers, Holland, Jermyn, and Walter Montague. The greatest damage she did to her husband was by persuading him to receive papal agents accredited to her court. Nothing inflamed public opinion more, nothing could have been more futile. Con and Rossetti were cultured, amiable men, but they soon found that Charles had no intention of changing his faith, that the Pope refused to make concessions (over the Palatinate and the oath of allegiance) and that a reunion of churches, occasionally talked of, was a chimera. It is hard to see what, apart from some money collected from Catholics, Charles had to gain from these negotiations, but it is obvious that they contributed substantially to the storm which was to sweep both him and his Court away. Nevertheless in this, as in many other matters, the civil wars were to be only an interruption. The same factors which produced the atmosphere of Charles I's court were to reproduce, in the Restoration court of Charles II, a stronger centre of Catholic and absolutist ambitions.

CHAPTER THREE

The English Revolution

IN the historical controversy over the causes and significance of the English Revolution, which has now continued for over a decade, increasing attention is being paid to the relation between developments in England and those in other countries where contemporaneous revolutions occurred – France, Portugal, Catalonia, Naples, Sicily and the Ukraine. The classical Whig historians treated the Puritan Revolution, as they called it, as something self-contained and unique because of the distinctive character of the religious and constitutional causes and developments which they emphasized, and which were not to be found abroad. Today most historians regard the English Revolution as part of a general European crisis; its events and their causes are no longer considered to be unique. For the English monarchy in the sixteenth and early seventeenth centuries can be described as absolutist, and the strains to which it was subjected and the opposition which it provoked were not very different from those which were to be found in contemporary France and Spain. One interpretation stresses the common effects on European countries of almost continuous war and intolerable taxation; if the burden in Britain was far lighter than in countries involved in the Thirty Years War, so Charles I's government was far weaker. Trevor-Roper has stressed the burden of expanded bureaucracies and expensive courts. The struggle between Parliament and Charles I has been compared with the attempts of representative institutions in European countries to defend their 'liberties' against royal or princely encroachment.

The group who give the greatest weight to the essential interconnection between events in Britain and Europe are those Marxists who see the general crisis of the seventeenth century as 'the last phase of the general transition from a feudal to a capitalist economy'. For them the English Revolution was the first 'bourgeois revolution', its success the most decisive product of the seventeenth-century crisis since it made the essential break-through by creating the necessary conditions for economic advance. This success of the bourgeois revolution led inevitably to English economic and industrial supremacy a century later, with its power to transform the world. It reflected the superior strength in the English social structure of bourgeois elements, landed, mercantile and industrial, whereas in none of the European revolutions were these forces sufficiently advanced to overthrow the monarchical institutions and aristocratic forms of feudal society which retarded political and economic progress.

This Marxist interpretation has stimulated discussion and provoked a great deal of criticism. The basic concept of a struggle between a Parliament representing bourgeois progressive forces and a King supported by reactionary, feudal interests and backward regions, has come under sustained and damaging criticism. The necessary connection between puritanism and capitalism has been questioned. Critics have asked whether there is any evidence of a direct connection between the 'success' of the English Revolution and later English economic growth and supremacy. Hobsbawm in stressing industrial factors, Hill in emphasizing the 'industrious sort of people' as the agents of economic advance, take less account than they should of the crucial importance of commercial forces, both in the opposition to Charles I and in the economic development of Stuart England. They also evade any direct comparison with what was, in my view, the area which most closely resembled England in every aspect of life – economic, religious, intellectual, social and political – Holland and Zeeland. According to Hobsbawm the Dutch was a 'feudal business economy', dissimilar to the English and therefore not comparable.* Hill rightly says that the Dutch republic and its civilization were taken as a model by those sections of English society which rejected French absolutism,

---

* This statement is based on assumptions, not demonstration, and its validity is increasingly questionable in the light of recent research. See particularly, R. Ashton, 'Charles I and the City', in ed. Fisher, *Essays in the Economic and Social History of Tudor and Stuart England* (1961).

but he has not fully developed or used the comparison in his published work.

Because of the nature of the subject, and in view of the amount of research which has still to be done, no more can be done here than to put questions and suggest hypotheses and possible lines of inquiry. First, it is vital to define terms of reference. What is meant by the 'English Revolution'? A clear distinction must be made between the three main phases of the period. First, the years of the Long Parliament and the civil wars, 1642–47, when the negative work of shattering Charles I's system of personal government beyond repair was achieved. Secondly, the period of intellectual ferment and social, political and religious experimentation, 1647–53. Of this phase, in particular, it may be asked in what sense, if any, it succeeded, since it was followed by the Protectorate. This can be interpreted as a retreat to traditional policies and institutions, but in the field of foreign relations it saw Britain as a great power exerting more influence in Europe than at any previous time in the century. In surveying these phases three questions have to be considered. What were the actual relations with European countries? What were the reactions of Europeans to developments in England? What was the attitude of the successively dominant ruling groups in England towards Europe, and what influence and practical effects did their policies and theories have on European rulers and opinion?

There is a further general question to be considered here and in other chapters. Did the 'English Revolution' succeed? Can it be regarded as conclusive in a positive as well as a negative sense? Everyone knows that the Restoration was inevitably incomplete, that it did not, and could not, restore the old order. But does this mean that decisive and irrevocable changes had already occurred, predetermining the outcome of the renewed political struggles of the years after 1670? Both Whig and Marxist historians have tended to assume that this was so, and skip lightly over the years until they reach the Revolution of 1688, a kind of postscript to the decisive, English Revolution. Such an interpretation ignores the strength of absolutist forces under Charles II and James II, all the more formidable because they had Louis XIV's government before them as an example. Indeed, it could be argued that the most immediately important result of the 'English Revolution' was to strengthen the forces of counter-revolution by giving royalist exiles first-hand knowledge of absolutist methods. Furthermore, the methods which had been used to destroy Charles I's absolutism were to prove a crippling handicap to the opponents of Charles II; everyone feared that if they were used again they would lead to the same results – civil wars and military tyranny.

The English civil wars coincided with the last stages of the Thirty Years War, but although most foreign states were absorbed in their own affairs England was not entirely insulated from its warring neighbours. The actual handling of foreign affairs by the Long Parliament and its committees is a subject on which very little work has been done, but it seems that three subjects occupied attention; attempts to get foreign recognition, the protection of the trade and shipping on which its revenues and war-effort partly depended, and the prevention of foreign intervention.* This was at times a real danger, but it should not be assumed that the readiness of foreign princes to send troops – for instance, Denmark and the Duke of Lorraine – was ideologically motivated; they traditionally supplied mercenaries wherever they were needed. French policy was at first limited to combating Spanish influence at Charles I's court, and to ensuring the supply of recruits for the French army which, surprisingly, continued throughout the civil wars. For a time the confusion in England entirely satisfied French requirements, but after 1645 Mazarin began to strengthen connections with the Scots as a precaution against the victorious Parliament. The Dutch were the most closely interested in, and directly concerned with, British affairs. The House of Orange was linked with the Stuarts by the marriage of William and Mary in 1641, which had been intended to increase its prestige and assist the campaign for the increase of its authority at the expense of the Republican liberties. In practice this sympathy for the Stuarts materially weakened the Orangists and delayed their plans. Frederick Henry and

* It is usually assumed that there was a grave danger of France or Spain intervening in the English civil war, but this aroused relatively little interest; it was rather the struggle of the Irish Catholics that engaged their sympathies and understanding.

William lent money on a scale which reduced their own resources. Their traditional supporters, the Calvinist ministers, were initially sympathetic to the Scots and the Long Parliament in their resistance to prelacy, crypto-popery and Spanish influence. The Regent class was alarmed, fearing that Orangist sympathies for Charles could lead to a naval war against Parliament which would be expensive and would expose their trade to attack. If successful, such a war would establish the House of Orange as sovereign, entailing the end of their 'true freedom' and heavier taxation, and re-establish Charles I who had tried before 1640, however ineffectively, to expand English trade at their expense. Naturally, they blocked all attempts at intervention and regarded the Long Parliament with a sympathy which later events were to destroy. This attitude, based like all Regent policies on commercial considerations, was misinterpreted by the parliamentarians, who were confirmed in the old country opposition belief that the Dutch looked on themselves as the main pillar, with England, of the Protestant interest in Europe.

Few Europeans outside the United Provinces understood the issues involved in the civil war, or knew much about the English constitution. Kings and their ministers, including even the Portuguese whose own rebellion had taken place in 1640, interpreted the civil war as merely a rebellion of subjects against their rightful sovereign. Catholics equated the Calvinist doctrines of Puritanism with the spirit of rebellion. The Huguenots, afraid of coming under renewed suspicion, urged the Long Parliament to justify its actions by some general Declaration to all countries. Certainly the example of the Long Parliament did have a direct influence on participants in the first Fronde, particularly the lawyers, who were encouraged to resist a tyrannical minister in the defence of constitutional and property rights. But it was not until the trial and execution of Charles that the attention of all Europe was turned to events in England, provoking almost universal horror and, it must be stressed, universal incomprehension.

The execution of Charles was followed by the virtual severance of relations with Europe. The Commonwealth Declaration of April 1649, stating that it would maintain all existing leagues and amities, met with no response. France engaged in an undeclared war from 1649 to 1653. It has been shown that although *parlementaires* often appealed to the example of the Long Parliament, the most frequent references to the events of 1648–49 in England which are to be found in the pamphlets of the Frondes were by Mazarin's supporters, who tried to frighten opinion with the prospect of similar developments in France. A few individual Huguenots looked to the Common-wealth for protection of their rights, as they had once looked to James and Charles as Kings of England, but they did not res-pond in any numbers to the unofficial approaches which were made by Vane and other members of the Council of State. In all Europe there is only one authenticated case of a popular movement directly inspired by events in England and appeal-ing for support on ideological grounds. This is the extremely interesting revolutionary group at Bordeaux, the *ormée*,* for whom, in fact, little could have been done, since the climax of their movement coincided in 1652–53 with the first Dutch war. Otherwise it is significant that it was precisely those groups who had had the closest connections with England who reacted most strongly against the regicide Common-wealth; for instance, Calvinist ministers in France, Holland and Scotland. The Dutch *predikanten*, previously sympathetic despite their traditionally Orangist connections, were converted into raging enemies of the Commonwealth, and there seems to be virtually no trace of sympathy for the new régime among the Dutch, despite the eclipse of the pro-Stuart House of Orange. Dutch recognition of the Commonwealth was due entirely to commercial prudence. The Spaniards, who also assisted the *ormée*, were the first great power to recognize the Commonwealth in the hope of gaining an advantage over France, but Spanish opinion applauded when royalist exiles in Madrid murdered the first Commonwealth envoy. Few Protestants understood the principles or practices of the Inde-pendents, and in Catholic Europe there was no understanding of the dynamic forces operating in England. Cromwell and the other leaders were caricatured as ambitious incendiaries, their religious faith dismissed as deceitful hypocrisy; the sects were equated with that universal bogey, the Münster anabaptists,

* The revolt was directed by popular assemblies meeting under the elm trees (*ormes*).

and religious and intellectual freedom denounced as a cloak
for licence, atheism and immorality.

On the other hand, most European rulers had only too much
reason to fear that their desperately discontented subjects
might be encouraged to rebel by events in England. Hyde, in
1650, predicted that the victory of the Commonwealth would
be followed by an attempt to 'destroy and extirpate all the
settled governments in Christendom'. But several factors
militated against the numerous rebellions of the time develop-
ing into revolutions which resembled the English. Most
contemporary rebellions were centred in the countryside, the
product of intolerable poverty and oppression, and were directed as much against the gentry as against the central authority.
Without positive ideas, and lacking any but local leadership,
such *jacqueries* were as negative and doomed to failure
as similar movements in pre-Maoist China. When popular
risings did receive effective leadership, it was supplied
initially by the parochial clergy and the preaching orders, as
in Catalonia in 1640 or in late sixteenth-century France; but
if they were to be consolidated they required support from
at least a section of the aristocracy, the class which in the more
developed countries filled the army, and in backward areas
still controlled feudal retainers. Now it may be said that
developments in Scotland after 1637, and in Ireland after 1641,
did not differ significantly from this pattern, but in England
two dynamic forces in particular converted a rebellion into a
revolution.

The first of these was the New Model Army, which was
unique in its composition and character, in that it was a professional but non-aristocratic force and that at least its cadres,
the volunteers as distinct from the pressed men, had a high
degree of political consciousness. The Army sought to serve the
interests of the nation as it saw them, as well as to satisfy its own
particular demands; whereas to call on the aristocracy for
armed service meant handing over control of a movement to
them – as the *parlementaires* found in both Frondes. Certainly
radical ideas and experiments would never have gone beyond
the stage of discussion had it not been for the Army. Among
these ideas the most revolutionary was the separation made by
radicals of the secular and religious spheres; a break-through

which led to the formulation of theories of political liberty, religious freedom and social reforms which were ultimately to have a considerable influence, for instance during the American Revolution. It also aided the establishment of an atmosphere of intellectual freedom, comparable to that of contemporary Amsterdam, which was to survive the Restoration; whereas in Catholic Europe the need to make a religion out of doctrinaire anti-Catholicism created new forms of intellectual intolerance.

The actual direction of foreign policy during the years 1649–53 was carried out by the Council of State; Cromwell and the 'grandees' may have had the ultimate authority, but they were absorbed by the Irish and Scottish campaigns. There are many questions about these years to which we do not know the answers. How serious was the interest taken in French affairs during the Frondes? How far was it political or ideological? How far did it follow the traditional line of concern for the Huguenots? There was a group, of whom Thomas Scott was the most prominent, who corresponded with *frondeurs* and favoured a Spanish alliance. Was this purely tactical and opportunist or the result of Spanish bribes, or was it based mainly on the hope of gaining commercial advantages over the Dutch? We know little about the discussions which preceded the St. John mission to The Hague in 1651 and his offer of union between the two republics, or about the attempts to obstruct Cromwell's decision to make peace with the Dutch in the winter of 1653–54. We know that the Commonwealth was being constantly exhorted to help European Protestants. How far did this develop into a concern for political as distinct from religious freedom? We know that some Levellers emancipated themselves from the religious fanaticism which coloured Englishmen's views on Ireland and upheld the right of the Irish to freedom; but even radicals seem to have thought that the destruction of popery was a necessary preliminary to the establishment of freedom in Europe, as the destruction of Laudeanism had been in England.

In later years the subjects of Charles II, humiliated by his failures and weakness, often made a comparison with the days when Cromwell, if a tyrant at home, had made Britain feared and respected throughout Europe. The classical Whig historians regarded Cromwell's foreign policy as his sole legitimate claim to greatness, and in periods of national crisis his strength, success and determination have been quoted – as, characteristically, by Winston Churchill in 1940. This picture cannot stand critical scrutiny. Cromwell, in the words of a contemporary critic, was 'not guilty of too much knowledge' in foreign affairs. His policies were misdirected, unrealistic and unsuccessful – indeed it can be argued that their failure contributed significantly to the Restoration. Cromwell's attitude to Europe remained that of an unfashionable, untravelled and rigidly Protestant country gentleman of the 1620s and 1630s, who had been alarmed at the advances of Catholic and Habsburg power and ashamed at having to remain a spectator while the Dutch resisted, and the great hero Gustavus Adolphus smashed, the forces of evil. Cromwell still lived in a world which had disappeared; the Dutch showed no enthusiasm for a union or even an alliance with him. None of the powers with which he had dealings – France, Sweden, Denmark, the Dutch and least of all Spain which offered him an alliance – still followed policies based on religious considerations. Cromwell remained blind to this. When discussing French affairs he still thought primarily of the Huguenots. Condé, the leader of the second Fronde, recalled to Cromwell the Huguenot hero of the sixteenth-century wars of religion, and he dreamt of his conversion to Protestantism. He approached Charles X as if he was Gustavus Adolphus. A principal motive for his celebrated intervention on behalf of the Vaudois was the fact that their persecution had been instigated by Henrietta Maria's sister. After the end of the fractricidal war against the Dutch in 1654 Cromwell now had unprecedented power; what he lacked was both knowledge of European affairs and the ability to profit from experience.

Both France and Spain had tried to obstruct the Anglo-Dutch peace, and both were aware of the threat to their own position represented by the English navy and army. Both powers made approaches in 1654, which had the effect of dividing Cromwell's Council into pro-Spanish and pro-French factions, in much the same way as in the days of James and Charles. Led by Lambert, the Spanish party emphasized the importance of trade with Spain, the offers of financial subsidies which Spain was making, the damage inflicted on trade by the French since 1649 and the aid and shelter extended to royalists by France. For Cromwell there were two fatal, if in practical terms irrelevant, objections. First, Spain would not concede the rights for Protestant residents which he demanded, whereas at this time Mazarin was respecting Huguenot rights. Secondly, an alliance with Spain would prevent him becoming leader of the Protestant interest in Europe, since Sweden and many Protestant princes were allies of France.

The general criticism of Cromwell's foreign policy has always been that he allied with the wrong power, a strong France which was to become an enemy to British interests, rather than a declining Spain which needed assistance. In fact there was no compelling reason why Cromwell should ally or go to war with either power. It should be noted that although he blundered into war against Spain in 1655, he was unable to conclude a French alliance until 1657; Charles II was quicker in reaching a formal treaty with Spain in April 1656. The Spanish war demonstrates Cromwell's lack of realism and obsolete viewpoint. The original plans for conquests in the Caribbean were directly inspired by the Providence Company of the 1630s which Warwick, Pym and other leaders of the parliamentary opposition had organized to attack Spanish trade, evangelize the Indians and settle pious emigrants. Its puritan colony had been wiped out, but Cromwell was easily persuaded that a strong expeditionary force would overwhelm the Spanish Empire. Thomas Gage, a converted priest and author of *The English American* (1648) wrote a memorandum stressing the religious benefits which would accrue; the conversion of the Indians who were ready to rebel, the punishment of the sinful enemy, the blow which Rome would suffer from the collapse of Spanish power through the interception of American treasure. The prospect of material profits was as alluring (and as illusory) as in the days of Raleigh. It was calculated that the expedition would cost little more than its maintenance at home in inactivity, that immediate profits in the form of booty would be followed by greatly expanded trading profits. The first campaign would see the conquest of Cuba and Hispaniola, the mainland would follow later.

These plans entirely ignored conditions in the Caribbean.

The results were pitifully out of proportion to the effort, Jamaica being at first of little value. There was a second and more serious miscalculation. Cromwell had not expected that the expedition to the Caribbean would involve him in a war in Europe. He thought that, as in the years before 1586, war could be confined to areas 'beyond the line'. The war in European waters required the maintenance of a large and expensive fleet for five years, and since the Dutch war had exhausted the Commonwealth's capital resources it necessitated heavy additional taxation. The Spanish Treasure fleet was twice intercepted, by Stayner and Blake, and the latter also established a remarkably effective blockade. But these spectacular successes, which have monopolized the attention of naval historians, went no way towards compensating for merchants' losses. Trade with Spain stopped, to the great advantage of the Dutch; assets in Spain were seized, and catastrophic losses were suffered at the hands of privateers operating from Dunkirk and Ostend and disposing of captured ships and cargoes in Dutch ports. Effective protection of commerce was lacking even after the capture of Dunkirk in 1658, which followed the Anglo-French victory at the battle of the Dunes. Apart from Downing, few appreciated the value of Dunkirk for the future, but were concerned lest it involve Britain in endless disputes with France, Spain and the Dutch. The war dragged on with no prospect of peace but, after the treaty of the Pyrenees in 1659 which ended the war between France and Spain, a very real threat of foreign intervention on behalf of Charles II. By 1660 the Commonwealth was identified with permanent war, extortionate taxation and anarchy at home. The mercantile interest welcomed the Restoration because it promised peace with Spain, lower taxation and the renewal of legislative action against Dutch trading interests.*

Charles II had been able to do little during the years of exile to recover his kingdoms. He tried to impede British trade in every way, suggesting to rulers that they seize the assets of merchants who acknowledged the Commonwealth, sending

* This feeling was expressed in a popular jingle, 'Make wars with Dutchmen, *Peace with Spain*, Then we shall have Money and Trade again.'

Sir Henry Hide (who was later appropriately hanged opposite the Old Exchange) to try to wreck the Levant Company's operations, and issuing letters of marque on an indiscriminate scale. Royalist privateers operated from French ports in 1649–53, Dutch in 1652–54 and Spanish in 1655–60. Charles offered his services to the Dutch, but they prudently declined them for fear of making Cromwell irreconcilable; however, he was permitted to establish an admiralty court at Flushing, presided over by the Bishop of Derry, of all people. But despite his political impotence Charles was persuaded by Hide not to place reliance on foreign intervention as the method of Restoration. As a result, in 1660 Charles was able without difficulty to repudiate the pledges which he had given Spain in return for hospitality and support. What Hide had not prevented was the indoctrination of the younger generation of Charles's servants and associates. Impressionable exiles, living in poverty, were naturally attracted by the power, prestige and wealth of the Catholic church and the absolutist systems of government; it is not surprising that they compared them favourably with the restrictions imposed by limited monarchy and anglicanism in the difficult years after 1660.

CHAPTER FOUR

The British and the Dutch

ELIZABETH, in her *Declaration* of 1585, referred to the Dutch as our 'most ancient and familiar neighbours'. The events of the following twenty years strengthened and extended the relationship. Apart from ideological considerations based on the shared experience of war against Catholic Spain, Britain's links with the United Provinces continued to be closer than with any other country. Trade provided the chief connection. The Merchant Adventurers exported large quantities of cloth, which constituted over 80 per cent of exports in the first decades of the century, to their staple at Middelburg for finishing and distribution. English, Scottish and Irish ports were always full of Dutch 'flutes', the recently developed class of ship which operated as universal short-haul carriers. During the season thousands of Dutch fishermen came ashore at east coast ports, particularly Yarmouth. Travel, on business rather than for pleasure, was on a large scale. Englishmen and Scots served in the garrisons of the cautionary towns or in the Dutch army. Sizeable English and Scottish communities existed in the big Dutch cities, and a large Dutch population lived in London. The ease with which emigrants crossed the North Sea in both directions, settled and were assimilated into the local population, is evidence of the similarity of the life, customs and composition of the English, lowland Scots and Dutch. The Pilgrim Fathers' fear that they, only one among many groups of religious refugees, would soon lose their national identity, prompted them to leave Leiden for America. In the previous generation, when thousands of merchants and artisans had left Flanders to escape Spanish re-conquest, religious persecution and punitive taxation, most had left for the Dutch cities, but a considerable minority had settled in London and East Anglia. That they made a distinctive, as well as demographic, contri-

bution to English life is certain, but this is a field which merits
further investigation.*

Despite language difficulties cultural connections were
strong and continuous. Dutch universities, recently established
and so free from scholastic and Catholic traditions, attracted
students, particularly of medicine and theology. Some Dutch
scholars, including Arminian refugees after 1618, worked in
England. Translated works of Puritan divines like William
Perkins formed a large part of the reading of the pious Dutch
middle-class. Books of all kinds poured into England from the
Amsterdam presses. Some were theologically or politically
subversive but the steadiest demand was probably for navigational and technical books. English readers gained most of
their knowledge of European affairs from the Dutch news-
sheets. Dutch artists of the second rank, such as Honthorst,
Mytens and Hollar, worked in England. Art collection was the
main motive for gentlemen to travel to the Netherlands. In
contrast, when sons of the Dutch ruling oligarchy, the Regents,
travelled, they did so for a characteristically more practical purpose, to form an understanding of the world as a preparation for
their part in public affairs. Unlike most Europeans they gave England as much attention as France; De Witt, for example, visited
England only six years before he became Grand Pensionary.

The course of domestic politics in each country was followed with close attention in the other. Englishmen un-
critically hero-worshipped Maurice of Nassau as a true son of
William the Silent. They generally accepted Oldenbarne-
veldt's condemnation as a traitor and this seems to have
stimulated popular fears of similar treachery in English court
circles. The condemnation of Arminianism by the synod of
Dort (1619) was used as ammunition for attacks on the English
high-church party. English divines were uneasy participants
at this synod; a more influential and forthright part was played
by the English ambassador, Sir Dudley Carleton, who had a
place in the States-General, *ex officio*. It would be valuable to
know more about both him and his equivalent in London,
Sir Noel Caron, who was a key figure in Anglo-Dutch affairs
until his death in 1624.

* This is one of the aspects of Anglo-Dutch relations on which it is planned
to organize research in the University of East Anglia.

The aspects of Dutch life which English observers chose to emphasize are revealing. They admired the practical and effective provisions for charity, town architecture and planning, the cleanliness of houses and streets, the banks and exchanges, the busy wharves, the rivers and harbours full of shipping. Unexpectedly they praised the Dutch countryside, neat and orderly, intensively farmed, bisected by canals, much of it expensively but profitably reclaimed. They envied the industry of the workpeople, the frugality of all classes, the universal devotion to business. Now these are commercial virtues and the pattern of life depicted was urban. Not all Englishmen sympathized; caste-conscious aristocrats despised the Regents as tradesmen and social upstarts, writhing in fury at the claim of the States-General to be addressed as 'Hogen Mogen' (High Mightinesses). Religious toleration, praised by Temple and Shaftesbury because it encouraged merchants, artisans and Jews to settle in Holland, displeased the clergy. Those who hated London were even more suspicious of its links with Amsterdam.

It is a dangerous simplification to over-emphasize the resemblances between Britain and the United Provinces. The basis for comparison was much narrower; it was between London, the Home counties and East Anglia on the one hand, and Holland and Zeeland on the other. London, the one great concentration of population, was to Britain what Amsterdam was to Europe, the great centre of trade and shipping, the chief market for food and consumer goods, the centre of finance. London alone had a tradition of municipal independence comparable to the Dutch cities; in London, as in Amsterdam, the choice and control of magistrates and militia officers was a crucial political issue throughout the century. In both cases there was a duality in politics, relations between London and Westminster (meaning both Parliament and the Court at Whitehall) were as intricate and important as those between Amsterdam and the Orange court at The Hague. Just as Amsterdam interests financed and so controlled the shipping of other ports like Hoorn and Enkhuizen, so London was pre-eminent in foreign trade. The surrounding countryside served the capital cities, while the larger towns – Haarlem and Leiden, Norwich and Colchester – contained the cloth industries, much of which had emigrated to both areas from Flanders.

In emphasizing these important resemblances two provisos must be made. London was not England. While Holland was economically independent from the other provinces and the major political force in the United Provinces, London could never depend upon influencing either court or Parliament. Trade was only a segment of a predominantly agricultural economy, and the fact that Britain had potentially greater resources than the United Provinces did not necessarily give London any advantage. Secondly, and more immediately relevantly, London was less successful even though it was the base for most of the new and expanding trades. Its merchants, captains and seamen invested money, ships, lives, courage and endurance in the dangerous and difficult trades to India and the East Indies, the Persian Gulf, Guiana and the Caribbean, North America and West Africa, on a far larger scale and with far greater eventual results than the grossly over-estimated ventures of the Elizabethans. In all these new trades, as in those long established, Englishmen found themselves in direct competition, and all too often in physical conflict, with Dutch rivals, and in almost every case they had to acknowledge Dutch superiority.

This conflict of economic interests with the Dutch was a relatively sudden development, and had far-reaching repercussions. The Dutch were capturing new markets and invading old ones, which meant that those classes and sections who most closely resembled the Dutch were also those most directly and adversely affected. The clash of material interests cut across religious and political sympathies.

The conclusion of the twelve-year truce with Spain in 1609 established the Dutch as an independent power. During these years of peace they gained a dominance over the carrying trade of Europe through the efficiency and economy of the flute as a cargo-carrier. It was on this dominance of European trade that their more spectacular but less important oriental and colonial trade was founded. They advanced their interest by establishing diplomatic relations with Turkey, Venice and Muscovy, and they virtually excluded their English competitors from the Archangel trade which the latter had pioneered. This Dutch ascendancy was in itself envied and resented in England, especially as it coincided with the serious depression which hit the cloth industry around 1616. Moreover, knowing that James was not in a position to put serious pressure on them, the Dutch were using methods which were bound to provoke English hostility. In 1616 the Dutch exploited James's financial weaknesss to obtain the transfer of the cautionary towns on terms very favourable to themselves. The Dutch showed themselves more efficient in the use of force, as well as in purely economic competition. Armed clashes in the Russian trade and the Spitzbergen whale fisheries ended to their advantage, but the most serious clashes occurred in the East Indies.

The original objective of oriental trade was principally spice from the Moluccas. In that region the Dutch, after ousting their Portuguese predecessors from the main centres, terrorized the native population into submission, and also seized English ships which tried to contest their monopoly. In 1623 they murdered a group of English factors at Amboyna after an odious semblance of a trial, preceded by judicial torture. This local victory in the Moluccas was consolidated by a more decisive success in West Java, in the strategically vital area surrounding the Sunda Straits which controls entry into the Java and South China seas. The Dutch used Jakarta* as their base, while the English operated from the native port of Bantam, and persuaded its ruler to attack the Dutch. In 1618 a strong force, under Sir Thomas Dale, was sent out from England but he failed to dislodge the Dutch or to build up a permanent base in the area. The Dutch success was due to the energy, ruthlessness and foresight of their governor-general, J. P. Coen, who was largely responsible for establishing an impregnable position in the East Indies. This was founded on Jakarta's central position, which was economically as well as strategically vital since it enabled the Dutch to gain control of most of the carrying trade between India and Ceylon, the East Indies, and China and Japan. This system of trade, roughly similar to that of the Dutch in Europe, employed the shipping and led to the accumulation of the resources which

* Known until 1948 as Batavia.

could be used for further expansion. Dutch trade and their
empire in the East were largely self-sustaining, whereas the
English were largely confined to the single long-haul trade
between Europe and India, and had constantly to send out
men and ships, besides bullion with which to buy Indian
goods.

Dutch success and methods in the East were deeply resented,
but news of the Amboyna massacre coincided in 1625 with the
need for a Dutch alliance against Spain. Similarly the resentment felt against the Dutch for another humiliating and damaging failure, the collapse of Alderman Cokayne's project, was
masked by the greater responsibility of James and his court.
Most English cloth at this time was exported as 'white', un-
dressed cloth, to be dyed and finished in the United Provinces –
the most profitable parts of production. In 1614 Cokayne was
given a monopoly on undertaking that only finished and dyed
cloth would be exported. His techniques and organization
proved to be defective, the Dutch prohibited all imports of
English cloth, and the total failure of the project deepened an
already serious depression. The old draperies never fully
recovered, and many export markets were captured by the
Dutch. Buckingham's wars also created new difficulties.
Although allies and bound by the treaty of Southampton not to
do so, the Dutch continued to trade with Spain. The French
war, in which they were not combatants, raised questions of
neutral rights at sea which were to bedevil Anglo-Dutch
relations for two centuries. The Dutch had to continue their
trade with Spain and France because their Baltic trade
depended on it, while the English tried to extend the list of
contraband, and their privateers used every pretext to make
prizes of Dutch ships. In addition the Dutch supplied France
with warships and munitions.

These issues inevitably weakened the former friendship
towards the Dutch as fellow-Protestants. English demands for
the redress of grievances and compensation for losses were met
by systematic diplomatic procrastination and evasion – eight
missions sent between 1610 and 1630 produced no progress
towards the settlement of differences. Existing conditions
clearly favoured the Dutch, who had a lead in every area
except the Mediterranean. Not surprisingly, suggestions were

made for the use of force – in 1620, 1631 and 1632 the court considered proposals for a Spanish alliance against them. But the effects of Buckingham's misrule, especially the state of the navy, made such proposals impracticable. How could Britain avoid falling still further behind? How was her wealth to be increased by the expansion of trade in the face of the existing Dutch superiority? These questions were explored by a whole succession of parliamentary speakers, pamphlets and books, which tried to provide the answers by combining examination of the reasons for Dutch success with analyses of our own weaknesses.

From Mun's *England's Treasure by Fforraign Trade*, written in the 1620s but not published until 1664, the problems were considered by Sir Thomas Roe, Lewes Roberts, Thomas Violet, Josiah Child and even John Evelyn among many others. Each had some special interest to advance, or favourite argument to emphasize, but they were in general agreement on the main reasons for English inferiority. The Dutch exploited every opportunity, whereas the lazy and poorly organized English neglected their formidable advantages. This was most apparent in the North Sea herring fisheries which were the foundation of all Dutch trade. The herrings lived in 'British' seas, yet our fishing industry was insignificant by comparison with the highly organized Dutch, and salted herring was always in demand in Baltic countries. The Dutch ascendancy in the carrying trade depended on two factors. The flute was cheaper to build and operate than British equivalents, and the pattern of Dutch trade was such that their ships rarely sailed without a full cargo. The Dutch stood at the centre of a two-way exchange in bulk commodities between the south and west and the north and east of Europe. From Spain, Portugal and Gascony they imported salt (for pickling herrings), wine and brandy, which were re-exported to Baltic countries. From the Baltic they imported corn, timber and naval stores, partly for their own market but primarily for re-export to the south. These were products always in demand, whereas English cloth was sensitive to trading conditions and fluctuations in demand. Raw materials for Dutch industry also came from abroad; timber for shipbuilding from the north; merino wool from Spain, coarse wool from the east, white cloth from England for the textile industry; iron and copper from Sweden, coal from England and Scotland. By contrast English ships, until the later development of corn and coal exports on a large scale, often had to sail largely in ballast since cloth was not a bulky cargo. In order to compete, England must also develop an entrepôt trade, and here progress was made in the 1630s with the development of Spanish trade and the re-export of colonial products. Legislation (as suggested in 1621 and passed in 1651) could be used to prevent the Dutch importing goods from other countries into England, but this was only half a solution if English freight charges continued to be uneconomical.

The more acute observers stressed the differences between a still largely agricultural England and a country where every aspect of life was directed towards the furtherance of trade. In Holland, as Child saw, merchants took an active part in government; every encouragement was given to new trades and industries and, above all, credit was cheaper. He and Downning argued that low customs gave the Dutch enormous advantages, the charges on raw materials and re-exports were only a fraction of those imposed in England. In the past high customs and misguided attempts to impose higher taxes on aliens had deterred Flemish refugees from emigrating to England. Trade advantages, not royal revenues, should be the first consideration; the King could be compensated by the introduction of excises, the taxes which provided most of the Dutch revenues. In addition Dutch commercial law was quicker and cheaper, Dutch merchants had banking, insurance and brokerage facilities, specialized warehouses, better commercial education, agents and factors all over Europe. One crucial advantage, not greatly stressed by contemporaries, obsessed as they were with exports, followed from their great and constant demands as consumers for commodities from their trading partners, such as Denmark, which had no other outlet. But of all advantages the greatest was their unique possession of ample capital resources. The Dutch could finance trade and industry at low interest rates, give customers long credit, export capital so as to gain control of sources of raw materials, buy in bulk, and support trades which needed large and continuous investment before they returned profits – like the East India Company in its first decade.

In Stuart England, as in most of the world today, the problem of how to accumulate capital preoccupied merchants and statesmen. In mercantilist terms the problem was how to keep in circulation an abundant and reputable coinage by preventing the outflow of bullion and by producing a surplus of exports over imports. Some believed that it was a matter of adjusting exchange rates, others of banning all trades which, like the East India, exported bullion. A crude popular view looked to the conquest of the Spanish Indies or the discovery of El Dorado. All luxury imports must be prohibited. State intervention and assistance in economic affairs was assumed, but in the period before 1640 royal intervention served private interests associated with the court and, apart from the ideologically unpopular Spanish policy, achieved little. The prosecution in 1619 of alien merchant-bankers for exporting bullion defeated its own object. Attempts to make the Dutch pay for fishing in the North Sea proved unrewarding. The failure to maintain the equipment of the fleet adequately, or to pay its crews, alienated the seamen and rendered it ineffective as an instrument against the Dutch.

The ineffectiveness of the monarchy was in sharp contrast to the attitude of the Rump, which passed and enforced the Navigation Ordinance of 1651 and refused to accept Dutch evasion and procrastination in the negotiations before the first Dutch war. Now many historians claim that the victory of Parliament in the civil wars represented the victory of those 'progressive' groups – merchants and shipowners, the navy, industrial entrepreneurs and workers – whose interests most directly conflicted with those of the Dutch. Again it is represented as that of those developed areas which I have compared with Holland. Is it, then, possible to describe the first Dutch war as a bourgeois war, one in which these groups used the power of the state to advance their own interests?

In general terms there is validity in these arguments, but important qualifications must be added. Mercantile interests and developed regions did provide Parliament with its main support, although not all supported its cause and many 'backward' interests and regions supported it as well. Mercantile interests demonstrably pressed for the Navigation Ordinance, but this does not mean that they controlled government policy, or that the Dutch war was solely one of deliberate, commercial aggression.

The situation which produced the Navigation Ordinance, one of desperate economic difficulties, is often ignored. Corn prices in 1649 reached the highest level in the whole century. Maritime trade was in serious difficulties. During the civil wars merchants had had to pay heavy taxation. They had lacked protection at sea because the navy was engaged in coastal operations, and in foreign ports because the Long Parliament lacked an effective diplomatic service. The seas were no safer after 1648 – besides Rupert's squadron, nominally royalist privateers operated from every point of the compass – Norway, Zeeland, Ostend, Dieppe, Jersey, Brittany, the Scillies, Munster and Scotland. France prohibited English imports and inflicted heavy losses (especially in the Mediterranean) in an undeclared war. In contrast Dutch prosperity was reaching a new peak. They were neutrals in the European war after making peace with Spain in 1648, when they also concluded a treaty with Denmark giving them preferential treatment in Baltic tolls. Dutch ships were gaining a stranglehold on all but the coastal trades; they were successfully invading the colonial trades with North America, the West Indies and Ireland; they had virtually excluded English ships from the Mediterranean and Baltic (in 1651 their ships were 50–1 in the latter trade) and in the Far East they were seizing English ships with impunity. Relatively, the English position had never been worse; all the gains which had been made in the years before 1642 had been wiped out, and the home economy had also been damaged by the second civil war and the wars with Scotland and in Ireland.

The Navigation Ordinance was intended to remedy this intolerable situation, by providing that goods could be imported only in English ships or those of the country of origin. This was aimed at the Dutch entrepôt trade, and benefited those groups (the Levant, Eastland and East India companies, and Trinity House which represented the shipping industry) which had made representations to the Council of Trade established in 1650. Imports from the colonies were reserved for English or colonial ships. We know comparatively little about its passage through Parliament, and the career of Oliver St. John, the man apparently most responsible for the measure, merits further research. The Dutch were quick to appreciate the threat which the ordinance represented to their trading interest, but they were slow to realize the determination and power of the Commonwealth to enforce it, and to assert its position in matters of general security.

Earlier in 1651 the Commonwealth sent a special embassy to The Hague led by St. John, after Dorislaus, its first envoy, had been murdered by royalist exiles. St. John was to seek a settlement of all outstanding issues in dispute, going as far back as Amboyna, but his main proposal was for a close union between the two republics, amounting almost to a confederation. This proposal was impracticable, but significant in that it reflected the traditional sympathy for the Dutch as fellow-Protestants which the parliamentary opposition had always felt, and which had been contained in the Nineteen Propositions, when the Long Parliament had demanded a Protestant foreign policy and a strict alliance with the United Provinces. It ignored fundamental differences and current difficulties. The Commonwealth was highly centralized, the United Provinces a loose union. The Regents feared that England would be the predominant partner, and that they would lose the independence which they had recently consolidated by the eclipse of the House of Orange. They feared involvement in England's European difficulties, for the Commonwealth was an outcast whereas the Dutch were at last at peace. The Regents had blocked all Orangist attempts to intervene in the civil wars, and in 1651 parts of Scotland and Ireland still held out for Charles II. Ideologically, the Commonwealth met with little or no sympathy. The Orangists were committed to the Stuarts, the strict Calvinists denounced Charles I's execution, and the Regents underestimated St. John. He had intended his proposals for union to help secure the Commonwealth by joining with the one potentially friendly power in Europe; their rejection showed that the only security lay in its strength at sea.

The first war was not the direct result of deliberate English aggression, but followed from Dutch miscalculations based on underestimates of English determination and power. The Dutch repeated the procrastinating and evasive tactics which had worked with James and Charles. They rejected St. John's proposals for union, and took no action to expel royalist plotters or arrest Dorislaus's killers. They made no attempt to meet St. John on old disputes. On the other hand the Dutch asked for freedom of navigation, and the special embassy sent to London in December asked specifically for the repeal of the Navigation Ordinance. The immediate cause of war originated in the undeclared war being waged against France. Dutch ships were being searched and cargoes seized, seriously impeding Dutch trade with France. While negotiations were taking place on the issue, the States-General ordered the fitting out of an enormous fleet of 150 ships. This was interpreted as intimidation. Tromp was sent into the Channel to prevent Dutch ships being searched. To the Commonwealth, determined to assert its sovereignty, this was an invasion of the British seas. An inevitable incident, off Dover in May 1652, precipitated war.

CHAPTER FIVE

The Anglo-Dutch Wars

GEOGRAPHICAL factors alone gave Britain overwhelming advantages in all three Dutch wars. Holland's economy would collapse if its trade could be paralysed, it would be unable to bear the expenses of maritime war, and unrest among the urban unemployed might explode into revolution. Its trade with Scandinavia and the Baltic was reasonably secure, but this vital trade was interdependent with that to France and Spain and could not continue without French and Spanish commodities. But the British Isles lay across the trade routes to the south and west. In the Channel, tides and currents, winds and navigational hazards, forced shipping to follow the English coast. The route around the north of Scotland was both longer and more difficult because of bad weather and dangerous coasts. The prevailing westerly winds gave the English another physical advantage. They enhanced the value of the concentration areas in the Downs and the Thames estuary and usually offered English commanders the initiative. The Dutch, in contrast, had great difficulties in joining up their main contingents each spring, or after dispersal by battle, since their main anchorages, the Texel and the Wielings, were over 150 miles apart. The shoals off the coast made these anchorages difficult of access, particularly in bad weather, but afforded the Dutch a refuge when pursued.* They also placed severe limitations on the design of Dutch warships. Shallow draughts meant that they carried lighter armaments than the English, and if the beam was increased to carry more and heavier guns, then their sailing qualities were affected. In 1652 only two Dutch ships had forty or more guns, while there were eighteen such ships in Blake's fleet.

---

* Charts, not maps of naval operations, should be used in class or individual study; for the Dutch wars Admiralty charts 1406 and 2182A are the most informative.

British privateers enjoyed enormous advantages in their attacks on Dutch trade. They had a far larger target to attack – as the Dutchman Pauw complained in 1652, the English attacked a mountain of gold, the Dutch a mountain of iron. It has been estimated that during the first war, between 1,000 and 1,700 ships were taken, while Britain lost about 200–250. In the second and third wars the ratio was less overwhelmingly favourable, but still worked out at more than three to one.* The English enjoyed other less obvious advantages. They had as much experience as the Dutch. Most officers had spent years at sea during the civil war, pursuing Rupert and operating against privateers. Blake, Monk and others, who had transferred from the army, proved remarkably adaptable. The Dutch had not had to fight or organize a fleet war since Tromp's victory in the Downs in 1639. Their navy had been engaged in attacking the Portuguese and in ominously unsuccessful defence of trade against the Dunkirkers. Theoretically they had an advantage in that volunteers manned their fleet, whereas the English pressed seamen and drafted soldiers, but in practice foreigners and landsmen had to be enlisted, and serious difficulties occurred with serving crews when new recruits were offered higher pay. Dutch naval administration often worked badly. Five separate Admiralty colleges maintained and supplied the fleet. Provincial jealousies hampered co-operation; Zeeland was usually late in its preparations, disrupting campaign strategy in 1665, 1672 and 1673. Significantly, the best equipped ships were the Directors' ships, provided by private enterprise. In the first war, at least, English administration worked with far greater efficiency and speed.

Not all advantages were on the English side. On crucial occasions the leadership and seamanship of Tromp and De Ruyter proved decisive, as when Tromp saved his fleet and convoy on the last day of the Channel fight in 1653, and when De Ruyter held off the allies in 1673. But the key to Dutch survival, and their most effective instrument of power, was provided by their economic resiliency and financial reserves. Dutch control of the seas in 1667 was directly due to their

* These are approximate figures; the whole subject of commerce raiding and protection is one that needs investigation.

The Anglo-Dutch Conflict

strength and Charles II's virtual bankruptcy; and the same
contrast of financial strength and weakness proved the decisive
element in the peace negotiations of 1673–74. In addition,
Dutch credit and economic connections won and retained
valuable allies. In the first and second wars Denmark, dependent on Dutch markets, closed the Baltic to all British trade, an
important factor since shortage of naval stores hampered
construction and fleet repairs. At the time of the first and
second wars France was also a trading partner, and her
friendship enabled the Dutch to drive the British out of the
Mediterranean in 1653, and to paralyse English trade during
the second. The closure of the Baltic and local superiority in the
Mediterranean could never be decisive, but they were obtained
with little effort, whereas British superiority in the decisive
theatre of the narrow seas had to be fought for.

The only certain way of paralysing Dutch trade was by a
close blockade of the focal areas off their coast. The Channel
fight of February 1653 taught the Dutch that even strong
convoys could not use that route, but their trade could continue by using the north-about route, which entailed considerable but acceptable risks. It ran far from the main British
bases, the prevailing bad weather facilitated evasion, and the
British lacked intelligence of Dutch movements. Homeward-
bound ships made for south Norway, where they would wait for
escort before sailing close to the Jutland coast for the Ems, and
so easily into the Texel. Outward convoys were a simpler
matter; they were heavily escorted as far as the latitude of
south Norway, and then left to disperse. Blake in 1652, Sandwich in 1665, failed to intercept such traffic, and the attack of
1665 on Dutch ships in Bergen also failed.

A close blockade could only be established after the main
Dutch fleet had been engaged and defeated, or at least damaged
and dispersed to separate bases. To seek out and destroy the
enemy fleet became the strategy of the British commanders,
although they repeatedly yielded to the temptation of trying to
capture returning East Indiamen, the richest prizes afloat.
When major battles were won, and close blockades established,
the results proved the correctness of this strategy; in 1653
Dutch trade was paralysed after the Gabbard; in 1666 Holmes
destroyed over 250 ships in the Vlie after the North Foreland

victory. But close blockades were more difficult to maintain than to establish; battle damage had to be repaired, wounded and sick put ashore, victuals and ammunition taken on. Bad food, disease and cramped quarters reduced the sea-keeping qualities of even well-found ships, and the prevailing westerlies increased the dangers of stranding on the shoals offshore.

The Dutch faced much greater problems. At first Tromp was given impossible directives, to protect unwieldy convoys and simultaneously engage the English fleet. After near-disaster in the Channel in 1653 he was freed to follow his own strategy of engaging the English fleet as the only way to safeguard trade. He challenged two set-piece actions. Twice he was defeated, as was Opdam in following the same strategy in 1665. Dutch ships and tactics could not ensure victory in set-piece battles. Smaller and more lightly armed ships led to reliance on fire-ships and boarding, but the English with bigger crews and heavier guns could usually hold off their enemies, and fire-ships were effective only against disabled ships. These limitations were eventually recognized by De Ruyter in his defensive strategy in 1673.

The early stages of the first war saw both sides make major strategical errors. Tromp was tied to escort duties which prevented him from destroying Ayscue's force when Blake unwisely divided his fleet. Political considerations led to Tromp's supersession by De With, and to the failure of many Dutch captains to support De With in the first battle, the Kentish Knock (September). This victory led Blake to overestimate Dutch losses and to undervalue their fighting qualities, so that he was surprised when Tromp sailed down Channel in late November, escorting a large convoy. Blake's weak and undermanned fleet failed to intercept and was severely handled off Dungeness.

The first major victory was due directly to the work of the Navy commissioners who provided Blake with massive superiority when Tromp returned with the homeward-bound convoy in February 1653. Tromp barely managed to save his force, but at the cost of critically heavy losses. Freed at last from merchantmen he sought out Blake in June, but received a smashing defeat (the Gabbard), losing at least seventeen ships; and his fleet was split into separate sections. The close English blockade, and the catastrophic effects it produced on the economy, forced him to challenge another action. Superior seamanship enabled him to reunite his fleet, but he was again defeated off Ter Heide, losing twenty ships, 4,000 men and his own life. The blockade was re-established throughout August. This made the Dutch situation desperate. De With managed to cover outward and homeward convoys, but at great risk, and individual sailings resulted in numerous losses. The English were actively preparing for 1654, and by March had 140 ships ready; the Dutch Admiralties, short of money and naval stores and beset by political differences, could not match their efforts. There was little prospect of their being able to challenge the English with any chance of success.

Despite this desperately weak bargaining position, the Dutch representatives at the peace negotiations maintained their rejection of a union with the Commonwealth, and were reluctant to make any concessions. At this stage the influence of the English commercial 'lobby' can be detected. It had not actually caused the war, but its members certainly wished to exploit victory and dictate terms to the Dutch. They strenuously denounced Cromwell for having failed in the peace of Westminster (April 1654) to satisfy British demands on the fisheries, the East Indies and other outstanding disputes. Cromwell, however, saw the Dutch as fellow-Protestants, thought that the world was wide enough for both nations, and wished only to secure the Commonwealth by depriving the Stuarts of any help from the United Provinces. He was satisfied when the States of Holland passed the Act of Seclusion (May 1654), barring the House of Orange from the stadholderate of the province.

The overwhelmingly favourable position of 1653–54 was what the sponsors of the second war hoped to gain, and they had clear ideas as to how victory was to be exploited. During the years 1654–60 the Dutch retrieved their commercial ascendancy, benefiting decisively from the exceptionally heavy losses (well over 1,500 ships) which English shipping suffered during

Cromwell's Spanish war. These losses, together with heavy taxation and political confusion, caused a severe economic depression. The speed with which a new Navigation Act was passed in 1660 demonstrated the seriousness of the slump and the determination of the restored monarchy to act with the same energy and methods as the Rump in 1651–52. This act was more easily enforceable than that of 1651. It was aimed directly against the Dutch. Enumerated commodities, especially bulky goods like wine and naval stores, could be imported only in English ships or those of the country of origin, and in 1662 their import from the Netherlands was specifically prohibited. Most colonial produce was reserved for English ships, laying the basis for the spectacular growth of the entrepôt trade in sugar, tobacco and dyestuffs, and an act of 1663 compelled colonists to buy most European goods in England. All foreign-built ships were registered, and after 1663 any that were newly acquired were deemed aliens. English ships had to have preponderantly English crews.

Commercial interests can be identified as calling for these provisions. In Parliament the lead was taken by Sir George Downing who had served Cromwell at The Hague, where he returned as envoy in 1661–62 and 1663–65. Downing has usually been depicted as the author of the second war, as the unprincipled agent of commercial aggression. This is a simplification. First, he found no shortage of commercial disputes, mostly deriving from the first Dutch and Spanish wars, which commercial interests urged him to press. Charles II demanded action against republican refugees and brought up the fisheries issue, while the rights of William of Orange also concerned him. Rivalry for Portuguese trade created new tension. For two years relations with the Dutch deteriorated, but an Anglo-Dutch treaty was unexpectedly concluded in September 1662, which provided for the settlement of all disputes. This was Clarendon's work. He realized England's weaknesses, that a war could not be financed until trade had recovered, and that retrenchment had reduced naval strength. He and Charles were aware of the danger of France intervening in an Anglo-Dutch war. For Downing these arguments were irrelevant. His policy of pressing the Dutch rested on the belief that they feared nothing so much as a war against England, knowing that defeat was certain. Under pressure they would eventually give way, but pressure must be exerted because of the weakness of the central authority in the United Provinces. Without it no redress could be expected, since most of the English complaints were directed against the virtually autonomous East and West India Companies, or the Zeeland admiralty courts. As late as 1664 when, after mercantile petitions, Parliament told the King that Dutch behaviour in India and Africa, and their failure to redress complaints, were the main obstruction to our trade, Downing continued to report that the Dutch were bluffing and would give way to pressure. It may be said, both of him and of the commercial interest in general, that they did not want war, but that they were not afraid of it should the Dutch prove obstinate.

Two factors made war inevitable. De Witt refused to appease. His firmness after 1660 had paid off temporarily in the treaty of 1662. In 1663–65 he was rightly convinced that concessions would merely produce mounting English demands. His French alliance, a well prepared navy and ample credit made resistance practicable. Secondly, there now existed a new and influential interest in England with openly anti-Dutch aims who also wanted war as an end in itself. This consisted of the court and navalist group, centred on James, Duke of York. James, as Lord High Admiral, personally concerned himself with naval questions, and hated the Dutch for invading English sovereignty over the seas, as well as for being republicans. He and his friends wanted active employment and the chance of glory. Former Commonwealth officers, grouped around Albemarle (Monk), wanted a return to service. Many senior officers, such as Spragge and Allin, had a piratical past as royalist privateers and were eager for prize-money. Politically, also, the advocates of war differed in background and motives. Some wanted war primarily as the means of destroying Clarendon, to use it in order to gain office or advancement. A small group of rising ministers had a more serious purpose. At this period, particularly in the France of Louis XIV, absolutism was being established and practised as a more efficient method of government than monarchy limited by representative institutions. In Europe, efficiency meant increasing military power for purposes of war and territorial expansion. In England (though not in Scotland) the army remained relatively unimportant; the would-be absolutists wanted to increase the size and effectiveness of the navy. Using this as an instrument of power, Dutch commerce could be destroyed. War would bring short-term advantages in prizes and an indemnity; over a longer period the Crown would benefit from the permanent diversion of trade and increased customs revenues.

The relations of members of this group to each other, and to commercial interests and issues, still requires further research. Clifford, unlike Ashley (later Shaftesbury), seems to have been more concerned with power than with commercial wealth. Buckingham had City connections, but it is difficult to say how far he or Rupert were seriously interested in commercial questions. James's own finances are an unexplored subject; but we do know that all sections – royalty, courtiers, financiers, merchants, shipowners and officers – were investors in the Royal African Company, and it was this company which actually precipitated the war. In 1661–62 the Dutch West India Company seized six ships off West Africa. The English company sent out Holmes to take reprisals. His capture of forts and ships in 1664 led De Witt to dispatch De Ruyter on a larger scale raid – a classic case of escalation. In the same year New Amsterdam, also controlled by the West India Company, was captured. In December, before De Ruyter's successes were known, Allin made an only partially effective attack on the returning Smyrna convoy. From then, until war was declared in March 1665, systematic attacks on Dutch shipping brought in over one hundred prizes.

Although the second Dutch war started with the highest hopes, adminstrative weaknesses were apparent from the beginning. Parliament voted the unprecedented sum of £2,500,000, but the money came in slowly. De Witt concentrated on a bold offensive strategy. Outward-bound convoys were prohibited from sailing so that seamen had to enlist in the fleet which was sent out to seek a battle. The result was the worst disaster of all three wars when, off Lowestoft in June, twenty Dutch ships were sunk or taken, and annihilation avoided only by the premature breaking off of the chase. But James failed to exploit his victory. The English fleet took valuable prizes during a cruise in the North Sea, but did not establish a close blockade. The attack on Dutch East Indiamen waiting at Bergen for escort was repulsed. De Ruyter returned safely after raiding the West Indies as well as West Africa. The summer ended ominously when administrative difficulties and the plague kept the English fleet immobilized while the Dutch established a brief blockade of the Thames.

This inconclusive campaign encouraged the potential allies of the Dutch. France, Denmark and the Hansa cities had expected them to be annihilated, and feared from the language of the English war party that Charles intended to establish a universal monarchy at sea to their own detriment. All neutrals were suffering from the drastic, uncompromising and corrupt actions of the English prize commissioners. Dutch resilience encouraged resistance, while the elaborate English diplomatic offensive collapsed in abject failure. In 1665, when it was already too late, Charles tried to construct an anti-Dutch coalition, sending envoys to Denmark, Sweden, Brandenburg and other German courts. Inexperienced and ill-informed, and often blustering and tactless, they had only untrustworthy promises of money to offer. Only the disreputable Bishop of Münster was enrolled, and attacked Gelderland, but his adherence alienated other princes. French obstruction was another reason for the failure, Louis fearing that any coalition might be used later to block his designs on the Spanish Netherlands.

The biggest diplomatic reverse was France's declaration of war in January 1666. Most ministers had depended on French neutrality, and had not taken French offers of mediation seriously. Louis had no intention of pressing operations against England, but fears that the French fleet would appear in the Channel led Albemarle to divide the English fleet. As a result in the Four Days' Fight (May), the Dutch severely handled their weakened opponents. Dutch merchant shipping sailed freely for a time, Zeeland privateers operated destructively from French harbours, and repairs took the English significantly longer than the Dutch. However, when the fleets fought again, off the North Foreland in July, the Dutch were driven back and 'Holmes's bonfire' saw the burning of over 250 ships in the Vlie. This was an illusory success. By the autumn of 1666 the Dutch still had reserves to call on but the English were on the point of collapse. Plague and the Great Fire had devastated London. Politicians were absorbed in recriminations and the intensifying struggle for power; public demoralization and corruption were general. The results are well known. There was insufficient money to set out a fleet for 1667. The Dutch, with De Witt personally overriding the admirals' objections, sailed up the Medway to burn Chatham dockyard. De Ruyter controlled the Channel through the summer. The war, for all the heroism displayed at sea, and despite unprecedented material efforts, ended in humiliation and the compromise peace of Breda.

The treaty of Breda was hastened by the French invasion of the Spanish Netherlands, and followed by the Triple Alliance with the United Provinces and Sweden. The revelation of French ambitions and power ended the period in which the Dutch could be represented as the sole enemy, and created a division of opinion and interests over the direction of foreign policy which was to continue until 1713, and is reflected in the controversial interpretations of historians. Morevoer there was now no opting out of the debate. Up to 1667 Britain need choose between a pro- or anti-French orientation only if she wanted an active European policy, but now the development of French policies affected British interests. Which should British statesmen regard as the first priority – continuing commercial rivalry with the Dutch, or the French military and diplomatic threat to the Spanish Netherlands? France was a logical ally against the Dutch, but the rapid growth of French sea-power created doubts, and Colbert's economic and fiscal policies were affecting British exports and shipping. Did this mean that France, rather than the Dutch, was becoming our most serious commercial and colonial rival? Or did the potential threat from France make it all the more important to consolidate our position first at Dutch expense, in order to meet this new challenge? If we allied with France there was the danger of being treated as junior partners, or even subordinates.

If we allied with the Dutch there was the prospect of becoming entangled in an alliance with other powers with whom we had few interests in common. If we allied with neither there was always a danger of France and the United Provinces joining together against us.

In the years after 1667 only one group had no doubts or hesitations. James and Clifford were determined to renew the war against the Dutch at the earliest favourable opportunity, and to profit from experience in planning a war of conquest. For them ideological considerations were paramount, their sympathy for absolutism and Catholicism led them to look on a French alliance as natural and logical. This would lead to the overthrow of the Dutch republicans and also enable Charles to become independent of his subjects in both government and religion. The secret treaty of Dover (1670) represents the logic of these arguments: a victorious Dutch war was necessary for their realization. For others, including Shaftesbury and the merchant interests associated with the Council of Trade, established in 1668, the Dutch were still the major obstacle to the expansion of trade. Current research may throw light on the very important questions of the attitudes of commercial and financial groups during the years 1670–74. Some seem to have supported the war throughout, but there was none of the enthusiasm and recklessness of 1664–65, and many were heavily damaged by the Stop of the Exchequer in 1672.

The Stop revealed how near to bankruptcy Charles was before the war even started. It involved the resumption of revenues which had been pledged to financiers to whom money was owed. Crown debts amounted to over £2,500,000 in 1671, and the money voted in 1670 for ships (to uphold the Triple Alliance) had been spent. The Stop freed the King's income, and he also had French subsidies, but financially the war was a gamble. It is not surprising that such emphasis was laid on securing prizes, or that in peace negotiations a demand was made for an indemnity by October, for without a quick victory Charles would be at Parliament's mercy.

Victory seemed assured. The last war had seen England isolated, the Dutch supported by allies; now the positions were reversed. Then the Dutch had with difficulty defended Gelderland against the Bishop of Münster, now they would be overwhelmed by the French army. In 1665-67 De Witt had remained in control of Dutch politics, but by 1672 his position had weakened and the Orangist Party was reviving. In 1665-67 the Dutch had barely held their own at sea, even with possible French assistance; now they would face an allied fleet in greater strength, and their trade would for the first time be attacked by French as well as British privateers. Victory was to justify the war, which had no intrinsically important causes. Ostensibly it was due to unsettled disputes over the East Indies and Surinam, and to revived English claims over the salute due to the English flag at sea, and the fisheries. These were pretexts. A special Dutch ambassador offered concessions on all these issues. The fact that, as in 1664-65, the formal declaration of war was anticipated by seizures of Dutch merchantmen and an unsuccessful attack on the Smyrna convoy, underlined the aggressive character of the war.

This initial failure set the note for the inconclusive naval campaign of 1672. The Dutch just failed to prevent the junction of the allied fleets. In De Ruyter's attack at Sole Bay Sandwich was killed and the largest English ship, the *Royal James*, destroyed, but both fleets had to withdraw for repairs. Subsequently the Dutch went on the defensive, having to disembark men and guns to help their army, and confining the fleet to convoy protection. The allies, after spending a month refitting, hesitated over their strategy. James, the enthusiast for total victory, wanted a decisive battle, although he could not provoke one if the Dutch stayed within the shoals. Shaftesbury, concerned with commercial advantage, advised the employment of the fleet to intercept merchant shipping, but the vital East Indiamen got home safely. Intelligence was received that the coast was almost undefended but no invasion was prepared. Bad weather and victualling difficulties impeded a blockade, and financial weakness led to the fleet being laid-up in mid-September.

French victories on land provided an alarming contrast. Their armies occupied most of the landward provinces, only the inundations saving Holland. These successes, and the use which Louis made of them, upset English calculations. In negotiating with the Dutch Louis increased his own demands, but made no real effort on behalf of Charles. The English claims, which Louis had earlier accepted, were for the cession of Brill, Flushing, Sluys and Cadsand. In English hands these would enable Charles to put pressure on the Dutch whenever he wished. Brill commanded the Maas, and the other three places would secure the opening of the Scheldt to English trade. This would re-establish old trading connections between Antwerp (which had never possessed much shipping of its own) and London, much to the detriment of Amsterdam. Louis did not welcome the presence of the English in these strategically sensitive areas. They might obstruct his future plans to absorb the Spanish Netherlands. He intended to use the neighbouring Generality lands, which he planned to annex, in order to reduce the United Provinces to a state of permanent dependence. The revival of Antwerp under English auspices would cut across Colbert's plans to exploit victory for the commercial advantage of France. Therefore Louis did not press English claims on the Dutch; instead he suggested the cession of the relatively useless port of Delfzijl in the north. The other English difficulty concerned William of Orange. It had been expected that he would welcome the defeat of the republicans and accept sovereign powers over a rump of the United Provinces. Undoubtedly Charles hoped that William would look to him for protection against excessive French demands and pressure, and would in return serve English interests. He could then be used to counterbalance the strong negotiating position which French victories gave Louis. William's refusal to accept this role placed England more firmly in the position of a subordinate to France, and ensured a prolongation of the war.

With the French held by the inundations, decisive victory in 1673 could be won only at sea. Parliamentary votes of supply were adequate for the equipment of a strong fleet. A clear strategical plan was prepared. The Dutch fleet was to be destroyed or dispersed, and an army landed. But despite a big numerical superiority the allies failed in the first attempt; De Ruyter delayed them by inflicting considerable damage in two defensive actions in the Schooneveld (June). The decisive phase came in August. An army of 6,000 men was convoyed from the Thames to Yarmouth where it stood ready for embarkation.

Thinking that the army was actually at sea, and invasion imminent, De Ruyter had to accept battle. If he was beaten then the army would invade. De Ruyter's defensive action off Kijkduin was both tactically and strategically a victory. The English did not again put to sea in strength. Failure led to bitter recriminations, Rupert, the seamen and all England (except Charles and James) putting the blame exclusively on the French. They were accused of having deliberately, as well as out of cowardice, evaded fighting, leaving the English and the Dutch to batter and weaken each other, to be 'gladiators for the French spectators'.

The eagerness with which anti-French rumours were accepted revealed the growing suspicions both of France and of pro-French elements at court. The thesis of the propagandist pamphlet published in March 1673, *England's Appeal from the Private Cabal to the Great Council of the Nation,* that the war had been designed to make France dominant, and that it was connected with absolutist and Catholicizing policies at home, seemed to receive confirmation. Furthermore, the war was becoming a general European conflict, into which the entry of Spain created serious problems. This would damage the one branch of trade which had continued profitably since 1672, and would reduce royal revenues. Despite this Charles stuck to his policy – for several weeks. In December he demanded Dutch recognition of English 'rights' over the fisheries and East India trade, and insisted that a settlement could be reached only at the general congress at Cologne. He tried to use the negative Dutch replies to persuade Parliament to vote money for another summer's campaign. Parliament's answer was hostile. Whereas in 1673 attacks had been directed against the domestic policies which accompanied the war, but not the war itself, now members denounced the war as a grievance and refused to vote money. £1,500,000 would be required for a naval campaign, but the revenues for 1674 had been anticipated. At the back of everyone's mind was the nightmare of the Medway; without a fleet some disaster would be inevitable.

No serious difficulties hindered peace. The actual negotiations for the treaty of Westminster in February took only a week. Such speed, and the actual terms, showed how thin had been the formal pretexts for the war. Charles gained only the salute to the flag and an indemnity, most of which had been pledged already.

If the second and third Dutch wars failed by a large margin to achieve their objectives, it has been argued that nevertheless they were an essential part in the process by which Britain overtook the Dutch as the world's leading commercial power. Another argument emphasizes the period of British neutrality in 1674–78, but most of the gains made then (for example in the Baltic where the Navigation Act had actually hampered British shipping) were lost after 1678. Geyl suggests that the French wars had a greater effect on the Dutch economy than the three Anglo-Dutch wars; while Charles Wilson finds evidence of real economic decline only after 1730, although the Dutch had been overtaken decades earlier. To suppose that British economic supremacy was based on naval strength or directly connected with Dutch decline, is to fall into the mercantilist fallacies common during the period. The whole question of the relative economic position of the two countries during the last quarter of the seventeenth century requires further investigation, and this must include examination of their social as well as economic structures.

In the existing state of the evidence it is possible only to ask a few questions and indicate some possible lines of inquiry. Is there any significance in the decline of Dutch cultural life, when after the flowering of art and architecture and a period of intellectual leadership, it became imitative and derivative, with the upper-classes (unlike their English counterparts) succumbing to francomania? In economic as well as cultural matters the Dutch were of Europe in a way that England was not. Their geographical position gave them advantages in European trade, and most of the commodities that they handled were of European origin or were oriental goods of a type traditionally in demand – although we need a new study of the English East India Company before we can begin to compare it with the Dutch company. Having in the first half of the seventeenth century created an ascendancy in European trade by a miracle of business enterprise, resourcefulness and industry, the Dutch were undoubtedly slow to adapt themselves to the changes which occurred in the early eighteenth century. Was there a connection between this failure and the inflexibility of the Dutch social structure? How important were the effects of Dutch investment in England? How and why did the Dutch lose the advantages which they had previously enjoyed in designing, building and operating merchant ships? One important factor was the rapid expansion of re-exports of colonial goods, especially tobacco and sugar, which required large numbers of oceangoing bulk carriers. This expansion was also connected with the revolutionary fall in prices of these previously luxury commodities, which created mass markets with low profit margins on a high volume of trade. The Dutch, with a tradition of restrictionist practices in luxury trades, and Amsterdam declining as an entrepôt, could not compete effectively. But after 1713 the French could, and the enhanced importance of colonial trade was bound to involve Britain in commercial competition and colonial wars with France.

CHAPTER SIX

Britain and France

To the British upper classes in the seventeenth century France
was the best known, most accessible and most frequently visited
European country. For them, connections and resemblances
with France were closer than those with the United Provinces.
Like Britain, France was a predominantly agricultural
country, dominated socially, economically and, at first, politically by the landowning class. Most gentlemen who travelled in
France regarded themselves, and were accepted, as equals to
the French aristocracy, and found a pattern of life congenial
to their taste – particularly as they usually travelled when
young and impressionable. The returned traveller who insists
that they order things better in France was a familiar figure long
before Sterne's time, and never have French influences and
fashions been more potent than in the years after 1660. The
French language was the most widely known among educated
people. It was in common use by the cosmopolitan society at
court. French literature enjoyed considerable popularity; the
Restoration stage was largely supplied with adaptations of
French successes. Poets and writers tended to employ French
words and phrases. Charles II's court, which always contained
many French visitors and exiles was dressed *à la mode*, listened
to French music, watched French ballets and was served by
French cooks, domestics, whores and physicians. Whitehall was
in effect a satellite of Louis XIV's court and reflected its life
and style. For every rather patronizing French visitor there
were many more impressed British visitors to the Louvre or
Versailles. Cadets of Scottish and Irish noble families followed
a tradition of entering the French service, in which they became almost indistinguishable from their French counterparts
from the poorer provinces.

This leads to an important conclusion. Whereas those
commercial and bourgeois sections and interests who most

closely resembled the Dutch were their direct rivals and competitors, there was no such direct or general conflict of interests
between the upper classes and France. Many who lived in
exile during the interregnum returned with a permanent
admiration for French ways of life, culture and government.
Moreover, until the 1660s there were also mutually advantageous and long-established economic connections. Cloth and lead
were exported in large quantities, wine and silk formed the
main imports, and English merchants and shipowners came
second to the Dutch in handling France's overseas trade. The
main ports contained prosperous English communities.

In addition to these close personal, cultural and commercial
connections, political relations during the first part of the
century were relatively friendly, although they were interrupted
by the unnecessary war of 1627–29, the unofficial war of 1649–
53 and the war of 1666–67 into which Louis entered reluctantly
and half-heartedly only because of his diplomatic engagements
to the Dutch. The old traditional enmity of the Hundred
Years War and Henry VIII's reign had been forgotten, and
there were no serious or chronic causes of conflict. The Restoration of a francophile King and court consolidated existing ties
of friendship. But this *entente* was not to last. Spread over
twenty years from the mid-1660s there occurred a significant
and general change in opinion, attitudes and policies. The
whole British relationship to France was transformed, so that
by 1688 all but a small minority were to regard French
political, diplomatic, religious, commercial, naval and military
policies as intrinsically dangerous or detestable, and as
constituting an intolerable threat to vital British interests.

The assumption of government by Louis in 1661 was followed
by an expansion of power which was unprecedented in modern
Europe. His spectacular successes explain the attraction of
absolutist methods of government to other sovereigns, their
ministers and dependents. We should not be misled by Whig
historians into believing that such methods were not only
abhorrent to Englishmen but also impracticable in British
conditions. Quite the reverse was true. What Louis accomplished was what Charles II's ministers and James II hoped or

tried to achieve, and the methods which they used were taken directly from the French example.

The primary achievement of absolutism was the establishment of national unity through the effective enforcement of royal authority. In France the pretensions of the great nobility and the lawlessness of the lesser had challenged the Crown; in England royal authority was limited by the King's dependence on Parliament – no sovereign before Charles had ever had to allow it to meet annually. In France, as later in Denmark, Sweden and Brandenburg, absolutism was based on fiscal independence. In the years before 1672 Charles and his ministers envied Louis the solvency – temporary as it was to prove – which enabled him simultaneously to construct a large navy, maintain the biggest standing army in Europe, build the expensive show-piece of Versailles, subsidize his allies and intervene in the affairs of other countries by bribing ministers, generals and ambassadors. Charles's political impotence, the failures of the Dutch war, and the mounting pressure on the Crown by the parliamentary opposition made such an apparently impregnable position infinitely desirable. For ministers, too, absolutism had compelling attractions. Their position of having to retain the King's confidence and at the same time satisfy Parliament, was always difficult and ultimately impossible, whereas in France ministers were responsible only to the King. Admittedly Louis treated them as subordinates, but Charles was too indolent, and James too limited in ability, to govern personally. In practice, irresponsible ministers would control adminstration.

There were other potential beneficiaries of absolutism. It would widen the career opportunities of the lesser nobility by expanding the small standing army. It would give increased opportunities and responsibilities to the professional bureaucracy which, recruited from the same social classes as the French *intendants*, developed rapidly after 1660. The financial associates of the Crown, such as Edward Backwell and Sir Thomas Vyner, who were harassed by parliamentary hostility, would gain in standing and security. Naturally all Catholics favoured absolutism. The aggressively anti-Catholic legislation of even the Cavalier Parliament showed that toleration could be obtained only by the suspension of Parliament and subsequent acts of royal prerogative. Moderate Catholics aspired to a position similar to that of the Huguenots in France, and some even hoped for reunion with the Anglicans; but the more militant hoped for nothing less than the conversion of Britain. They calculated that royal absolutism could be followed by the use of methods which had been proved abroad. An absolute King could make systematic use of patronage, impose civil disabilities and differential taxation on stubborn Protestants, give religious orders control over education and, eventually, employ military force and physical terrorism.

All absolutist elements were naturally connected with the court, and constituted only a minority of the 'political nation' in England, though perhaps not in Scotland. However even before popular fears of absolutism became acute, at the time of the Cabal ministry, developments in France were making an impact. After 1664 the practical effects of Colbert's policies began to affect many vital British interests.

The most astonishing and alarming development was the sudden and spectacular creation of a formidable French navy. Before 1662 French naval strength was negligible; less than £25,000 had been spent on it each year. By 1670 Cobert was spending nearly £1,000,000 a year, and his strict supervision and control ensured that this massive expenditure produced results. The fleet became the equal of the English and Dutch in numbers, and their superior in quality. Unlike its rivals it consisted almost entirely of new ships, bigger, more heavily armed and better designed, supported by efficient dockyards and arsenals. Naval schools were founded to train officers, and a system of registration and periodical service, the *inscription maritime*, replaced the haphazard impressment of seamen. New bases were built – Brest, and the entirely new port of Rochefort, which greatly impressed Locke. Existing bases were equipped with new defences. Colbert's naval achievements transformed the whole relationship between France and Britain; the only parallel is the similar work of Tirpitz in the years before 1914. And, as in the latter case, this alarming increase in naval strength was being developed by what was already the most powerful military state in Europe. The French army, organized by Le Tellier, Louvois and Martinet, led by Turenne and Condé, provided Louis with an unequalled instrument of power. It was far stronger and more capable of sustained offensives than the army which had beaten Spain in the 1650s. Its effectiveness was first demonstrated in 1667, when its campaign in the Spanish Netherlands upset the European balance of power, and put an area of vital importance to Britain at Louis's mercy.

The French diplomatic service provided Louis with an instrument of policy which was hardly less effective. He was the best informed man in Europe. At every court his ambassadors and envoys had long-established connections, and clandestine contacts, which enabled them to influence policy decisions and intervene in domestic politics, particularly in those countries which had representative institutions. The objectives of such intervention in Britain were surprisingly limited. Whig historians, arguing from the assumption that Louis aimed at the 'domination' of Western Europe, believed that he wished to control British affairs and use Charles, James and their ministers as puppets. This is to overestimate Britain's importance in French eyes. Louis had little interest in British affairs as such, as he was to show in 1688. His experiences in 1670–74 gave him a low opinion of Britain's value as an ally, and until Marlborough's victories Britain was not impressive as an enemy. For most of his reign Louis aimed to neutralize Britain at minimum cost – he was never lavish with subsidies or bribes – by exploiting her many weaknesses. Royal poverty led to the French purchase of Dunkirk in 1662; the corrupt appetites of ministers made their purchase equally easy. Opposition factions appealed to Louis for support in 1678 and 1680, and Charles himself was constantly applying to the French ambassador. Louis usually had a choice of policies; either to rely on the King, his cousin, or to perpetuate the confusion into which political affairs so easily and frequently collapsed. Both courses entailed risks: Charles proved himself to be unreliable and there was a constant danger that support for the opposition might drive ministers into joining with William of Orange.

In European courts French diplomats generally outmatched Dutch, Imperial and Spanish representatives and totally eclipsed English diplomats – when they existed. The latter suffered from frequent political changes at home, and their poverty reflected that of their master. Ignominious failure usually resulted when they were instructed to oppose French influence; attempts in 1665–66 and 1680–81 to construct anti-French coalitions failed completely. Occasional successes were achieved, the most important being Sandwich's commercial treaty with Spain in 1667, and his mediation of peace between Spain and Portugal in 1668, despite French obstruction.

The fourth development in France, the systematic expansion of shipping, trade and industry organized and fostered by Colbert, must be directly related to the growth of French sea-power. In Colbert's eyes they were complementary; economic affairs were a matter of state, the ultimate purpose was to mobilize the increased wealth which economic expansion would produce for the service of the King. Power, not prosperity, was the aim. Therefore his achievements were not only economically damaging for Britain, but politically dangerous. Contemporaries believed that France was becoming wealthier at our direct expense, and that this must mean that France was becoming stronger and Britain increasingly enfeebled. The terms of trade were changing to our grave disadvantage, and unless a commercial treaty could be negotiated the British position must continue to deteriorate.

Three points need emphasis on this very important subject. First, Colbert's commercial policies were aimed primarily and avowedly against the Dutch, who had a far greater share of French trade; but when enforced they had a much more serious effect on the economy of Britain than on that of the United Provinces. Dutch efficiency and economic strength were such that many of Colbert's projects, the *Compagnie du Nord*, for instance, collapsed in competition against them, and he found that France could not dispense with Dutch merchants, ships and imports, even during the war of 1672–78. But the effects on English textiles were serious. In a few years the textile industries which Colbert encouraged and subsidized were able to supply most French requirements, and enabled him to impose high tariffs on English goods. Secondly, the English cloth industry was widely dispersed over the country, and the depression created by Colbert's tariffs was bound to affect many sections of the nation. Members of the landed gentry, whose rents (and poor rates) were affected, voiced their resentment in Parliament, where the textile areas were if anything over-represented. Unemployment also created serious dangers of riots, particularly in 1670, when there was already widespread resentment against the Conventicle Act. Thirdly, the beginning of economic resentment against France coincided in time with the pro-French foreign policy of the Cabal, and certainly helped to undermine policies which were already suspect on political and ideological grounds. The Cabal claimed to be representing merchant interests in going to war against the Dutch, but its failure to persuade the French to reduce their tariffs helped to discredit them. As an M.P. commented: 'Fifty per cent upon our goods in France, and yet the war with Holland upon account of trade.'

The first important protective measure had been Fouquet's duty on foreign ships in 1659. In 1664 Cobert issued his first tariff for the *cinq grosses fermes*; duties went up by about 14 per cent, but the improvements which he made to the administrative machinery of enforcement were more important. These made the duties of 1667 virtually prohibitive, and in addition English merchants complained that inspectors used regulations to hamstring their trade. In the negotiations of 1668–69 the English asked for the withdrawal of these new duties, but without effect. In 1672–74 they failed even to secure the resumption of negotiations, and an agreement finally concluded in 1677 dealt only with maritime questions. Predictably, Parliament reacted strongly. Besides listening sympathetically to the complaints of single trades and interests, it concentrated attention on the general effect of Colbert's economic and fiscal policies, that the fall in exports greatly aggravated an already unfavourable balance of trade with France. In 1674 a group of leading merchants produced a statement, the Scheme of Trade, which estimated the annual deficit as £965,128. The consequent outflow of bullion, it was believed, was responsible for the scarcity and poor quality of the currency, for the difficulty of raising taxes, for a fall in rents, and it enabled Louis to finance his war-effort against most of Europe.

At first many merchants who were engaged in the French trade argued that pressure, in the form of moderate tariffs on French goods, would produce concessions. The Commons referred the Scheme of Trade to a committee, whose chairman was the old opponent of the Dutch, Sir George Downing. In October 1675 it was resolved that a bill should be introduced prohibiting all French commodities unless French tariffs were reduced to the rates of 1660. The subsequent negotiations produced only the maritime agreement of 1677. This agreement gave English ships considerable advantages while the European war continued – a move intended by Louis to alarm the Dutch, whom he continued to regard as much more important than the English. In 1678, in order to persuade the Dutch republicans to force William to make peace, Louis freed Dutch traders and imports from the high tariffs of 1667. This left their English competitors at a permanently hopeless disadvantage, and led to immediate retaliation. In 1678 Parliament prohibited all imports of French wine, silk, linen, cloth, salt and paper; goods which could be dispensed with as they were all luxuries or procurable elsewhere.

Of course the general picture of economic relations with France which Parliament accepted, and the figures of the unfavourable balance of trade, were simplifications. French tariffs were blamed for the decline of inefficient and obsolescent industries – bay manufacture for instance – and for entirely unrelated economic and social changes. During the last years of the reign exports to France of finer quality textiles began to recover, and in 1685 James II's 'loyal' Parliament removed the prohibitions on French imports. It may be significant that merchant interests were weakly represented in this House of Commons.

The final cause of the deterioration in Anglo-French relations was colonial rivalry, especially in the Caribbean. By 1666 the Dutch had been largely excluded from trade with the English plantations, sugar exports to England, and re-exports to Europe, were increasing, and it was claimed that over 400 ships and 10,000 seamen were employed in the West Indian trade. The increased demand for slaves was responsible for the rivalry in West Africa which led to the second Dutch war. This war proved to be disastrous. The Dutch took Surinam, but more ominously, and destructively, the French captured Antigua, Montserrat and St. Kitts. In 1666-67 Harman struck back at French shipping, but this first of the long series of

campaigns for the sugar islands left the English colonies
enfeebled. Colbert's emphasis on West Indian trade was
important for the future. Peaceful competition and wars with
the Dutch had mainly concerned European trade; the wars
against France in the eighteenth century were to be, in part,
for the increasingly important colonial trades.

The French invasion of the Spanish Netherlands in the
spring of 1667 was a crucial event both for British and for
European history. It demonstrated to all the crushing power
of the French army, and the fact that this territory was now
entirely at the mercy of France. Neither the English nor the
Dutch could permit the absorption of the Spanish Netherlands
by Louis, and clearly his 'devolutionary' claims on behalf of
his Queen were only a preliminary to the annexation of the
whole area. Yet how could these states, neither of them military powers, check Louis? The Emperor was concerned with his
eastern frontiers, and in 1668 concluded a secret partition
treaty with France. At any time after 1667 Europe could find
itself suddenly plunged into a general crisis over the Spanish
inheritance, with Louis in a strong position to assert his claims.

The Whig historical tradition decreed that the preservation
of a balance of power in Europe, and the protection of the
integrity of the Low Countries, were essential constituents of
English foreign policy. Louis, with Philip II and Napoleon,
was regarded as one of those who threatened these national
interests and had to be resisted. Consequently Macaulay,
Hallam and Trevelyan condemned the attitude of Charles II
and James II as corrupt, immoral and contemptible, a betrayal of national interests for personal pleasure, dynastic
considerations and Catholicizing policies, in shameful contrast
to William III's consistency and endurance. Religious motives
led Catholic historians to disagree, and in the 1920s another
group of writers presented a reassessment of Stuart foreign
policy. Influenced by the *entente* and wartime alliance with
France, they argued that similarly in the seventeenth century
there had been no essential conflict of interests between
Britain and France, and that (as in the later case of Kaiser
Wilhelm's Germany) the real enemy had been our commercial

and naval rivals, the Dutch. Arthur Bryant argued that Charles, in strengthening and valuing his ties with France, was following the traditional policy of Elizabeth and Cromwell, and that it was the selfishly factious opposition whose behaviour was anti-national. C. H. Hartmann claimed that Charles, thinking of safeguarding our sea-power and commerce, would not ally with France until Louis recognized his supremacy at sea. According to his thesis French and English interests did not conflict, the French being a military power with continental ambitions, whereas the Dutch were the colonial rivals Charles had to beat in order to lay the basis of the British Empire. These arguments cannot stand detailed examination.* Past alliances with France had had as their object protection against a powerful Spain, which had almost collapsed after 1659. Charles's representations did not check the expansion of French sea-power, indeed he could not significantly influence French policies at all, the inevitable fate of any statesman who supports another country because it is strong. Certainly the Opposition included most disreputable and dishonest men, but Charles's conduct made him universally distrusted, abroad as well as at home. The Stuart apologists all completely ignore the aims, progress and effects of Cobert's work, which was making France, rather than the Dutch, our principal naval, commercial and colonial rival.

The English response to the French offensive of 1667 was to negotiate with both the Dutch and the French. The latter contemptuously under-valued English friendship, which gave Arlington and Temple an opportunity to close with De Witt, and to conclude the Triple Alliance with the United Provinces and Sweden in January 1668. Contemporaries then, and historians since, generally interpreted this alliance as a sharp check to French ambitions, but neither Arlington nor De Witt saw it as an anti-French move. They were concerned to assert a claim to be consulted in deciding the future of the Spanish Netherlands. Eventually, given Louis's ambitions, this must lead to conflict with France, but at the time the purpose of the Triple Alliance was not to fight France – unless

* Academic historians have usually dismissed them out of hand, but Bryant's and Hartmann's works did have the merit of being based on manuscript material, some of it new.

Louis tried to seize the whole country – but rather to coerce Spain into a compromise settlement which would end the fighting before it could lead to further French advances or general war. Spanish pride, and Swedish dependence on Spanish subsidies, rendered this task difficult. Temple, one of the heroes of Whig history and an able diplomat whose career needs reassessment, was closer to the Imperial diplomat, Lisola, who wished to extend the Triple Alliance into a general and avowedly anti-French coalition, but he had little influence at court. Charles acted in an opportunist manner. He used the alliance to get money out of Parliament, and also to persuade Louis to pay an adequate price for an English alliance. With James and Clifford already eager for another war against the Dutch, Arlington quickly abandoned the Triple Alliance, to become one of the signatories of the secret Treaty of Dover in 1670.

This diplomatic change of front was essentially ideological and personal in motivation, the work of a small court group; James, Clifford, Arlington, Arundel of Wardour and Charles. The treaty provided for French subsidies to Charles, reserved command at sea for an English admiral and defined English annexations from the Dutch. Charles announced that he would declare himself a Catholic, with the French responding with the promise of 6,000 soldiers to suppress any popular disturbances. This was naturally omitted from a second secret treaty, the 'simulated' treaty signed by the Protestant ministers, which fixed the beginning of the war for spring, 1672. The double deception involved in these treaties has always been condemned on moral grounds, and they were also to be condemned by the failure of the third Dutch war. There is a third objection. Charles was not, as Stuart apologists have contended, negotiating with Louis on terms of equality; he was not even accepting the position of *the* client, but of *a* client of France. For Louis the Dover treaty was merely part of his general preparations for war, and it put Britain on the same level as Sweden or Cologne.*

The terms of the Dover treaty remained a secret, but the effects soon made themselves obvious in the policies of the

* The true relationship of Britain to France is reflected in the surprisingly small amount paid in subsidies by Louis; in 1671–77 they totalled £750,000; in 1681–85 £400,000.

Cabal, and in the Dutch war. Charles, James and the court
became identified with the French interest, an identification
which was strengthened by the criminally provocative
Modenese marriage which Louis helped to arrange for James.
Such marriages, as M.P.s commented, were the reason why
popular fears of popery were reviving so strongly. In the years
after 1674 the Opposition frequently attacked France, calling
for the withdrawal of all British mercenaries serving in the
French armies, and working closely with the Dutch, Spanish
and Imperial ambassadors or ministers. Debates on foreign
affairs greatly embarrassed the new Lord Treasurer, Danby.
For more than five years, from 1673 until early 1679, he
survived the difficulties of satisfying both a francophile court
and a francophobe Parliament and country. His own inclination was to build an understanding with William, but financial
pressure also compelled him to negotiate with France, for
subsidies. He had to satisfy Barrillon, the French ambassador,
that Britain would remain neutral, and simultaneously persuade Parliament that he intended to follow a vigorously anti-
French policy. Like most informed persons outside the court
he was alarmed by the continued advances of the French
army; by early 1677 they had penetrated into the heart of the
Spanish Netherlands and, despite William's tenacious if
clumsy resistance, seemed poised to overwhelm the whole
territory. William, the Emperor, Spain and the other Confederates pressed for English intervention as a last resource. And
when Danby negotiated the marriage of William to Mary
(November 1677), concluded a treaty with the Dutch (January
1678), landed troops at Ostend and asked Parliament for
supply to set out a fleet and equip an army, it seemed as if
Britain would re-enter the war as an enemy of France.

The way in which Louis countermined Danby, William and
the Confederates during 1678 shows the power and effectiveness of his diplomacy. In Holland the French ambassador
played on suspicions of Charles's sincerity and scepticism of
his ability to finance a war. He intervened in Amsterdam
politics, and played on fears that William wished to become
sovereign. In England Barrillon now bribed the more extreme
opposition members in the Commons to obstruct the supply
which Danby requested. They alleged, and some may have

believed, that the army was intended for use at home in suppressing liberties, not for employment abroad against France. Their willing acceptance of French money, and their systematic obstruction of a war for which they had called earlier, was as unprincipled as the conduct of Charles which they continued to denounce. Some of these men were entirely self-seeking, others were opportunists who would accept aid from any source in order to destroy Danby. Barrillon achieved this in the last session of the Cavalier Parliament. With his assistance members produced secret correspondence which showed that when he had been asking for money for an army, Danby had been simultaneously negotiating with France for subsidies in return for neutrality.

The French succeeded on all fronts. Obstruction of supply prevented English intervention in the war. The Amsterdam republicans forced the States-General to conclude a separate peace at Nijmegen, abandoning the Confederates who had to negotiate singly with France. This disintegrated the coalition, while Danby's fall and the dissolution of the Cavalier Parliament plunged England into the confusion of the Exclusion crisis which European statesmen interpreted as the prelude to another civil war. When, in 1680, for tactical reasons Charles and Sunderland tried to form a general alliance, they returned negative or evasive answers. Only the desperately weak Spaniards concluded a treaty of mutual assistance. Halifax, Temple and other ministers intended this to act as a guarantee for the Spanish Netherlands, but Charles expected that it would persuade Louis to buy him off. At first, in 1679 and 1680, Louis rejected his appeals, having no close interest in English politics as such, but being concerned only to neutralize England during his next round of territorial advances, the *réunions* of 1679–83. When, in 1681, Louis did finally agree to give Charles subsidies on condition that Parliament was not allowed to sit, so ensuring that he could not go to war, it was only because it began to appear that the intensifying Exclusion crisis would eventually lead to William's becoming Regent.

The Exclusion crisis, apparently based on hysteria and lies, cannot be understood without reference to developments in France. The 'French at Whitehall', the group of pro-Catholic and absolutist-minded courtiers, were feared because they had

Louis behind them. The one piece of irrefutable evidence of
the Popish Plot, Coleman's secret correspondence with La
Chaise, linked the two sources of danger; Coleman served
James as parliamentary agent and general contact man; La
Chaise, a Jesuit, was confessor to Louis and a zealot for the
persecution of the Huguenots. In pamphlets, election speeches
and petitions, the Whigs referred to the menace from France
and French principles, describing conditions there as a fore-
taste of what England must expect under a Catholic and
absolutist King. Although the Whigs were eventually defeated,
their arguments were to survive for a century. The famous
slogan, 'No Wooden Shoes!', expressed the belief that absolutism and poverty went together. A sombre picture was given of
life under Louis: persecution or legal chicanery directed against
the Huguenots, an abjectly broken and miserable peasantry, a
richer and even more arrogant clergy, a luxurious and expensive court, a nobility reduced to servile dependence and, re-
awakening memories of the interregnum, the use of the army
in domestic politics. The Whigs paid little attention to the
detail of foreign policy, preoccupied as they were with the
struggle to pass Exclusion, but all their fears of absolutism
were based on its success in France.

Quite apart from the readiness of many Whigs to accept
French bribes, it would be a simplification to describe the court
as pro-French and the Opposition as anti-French. In Charles's
last years the court contained ministers (notably Halifax) who
distrusted James and wished to join with William in checking
French advances in Europe. Charles used them to counterbalance James, but their attempts to initiate an active European
policy lacked reality since this would necessitate the calling of
Parliament. French subsidies were paid only on condition that
no Parliament was summoned, and when James succeeded in
1685 he actually apologized for having called one before
consulting Louis. At first the pattern of the previous reign was
repeated. James appealed for regular subsidies, hinting that
without them he might be forced to follow an anti-French
policy; this was the purpose of his renewal of existing treaties
with the United Provinces in August. However it would be

entirely wrong to regard James as a French puppet. His early appetite for money was based on the unfounded fear that Parliament might restrict supply, but its votes in 1685 made James independent both of extraordinary taxation and of French subsidies, which had amounted to only around £50,000, mostly arrears owing to Charles. James was not subservient by nature. His domestic policies absorbed almost all his attention, and as the resistance provoked by them increased so James had even less time and inclination for European affairs – an important factor contributing to William's success in 1688. Like Charles I in 1629–40, James turned away from Europe, but two European developments helped materially to destroy him and his policies.

First, in the years 1687–88 Europe was moving inexorably towards another general war. Louis calculated, and William feared, that Britain was bound to become involved on the French side. James refused to face this danger; negotiations showed that Louis would offer quite inadequate subsidies unless James bound himself to France, in effect as a subordinate. A French alliance meant war, and this would necessitate parliamentary votes of supply, which were likely to be granted only on conditions which would wreck the King's domestic policies. These policies were also producing a continuous deterioration of relations with the Dutch. They provoked an angry propaganda war. James protested against the activities of political refugees in the United Provinces, and was afraid that they were influencing the English and Scottish regiments in Dutch service. When William rejected his request for their repatriation, James issued a Proclamation ordering both officers and men to desert. He also ordered Dutch ships to be searched for English seamen, which would have provoked serious incidents had it been enforced. In both countries naval armaments were being prepared, and for a time in the spring of 1688 it seemed that the fleets might clash in a crisis which developed between Denmark and Sweden, with the English supporting the former as the ally of France.

The second development, while less directly a cause of William's invasion, had more important effects on British opinion. This was the Revocation of the Edict of Nantes by Louis in October 1685. Its effects can be compared only with

those of Alva's persecution in the Netherlands a century earlier.
The Huguenots who suffered from the Revocation were the
foreign Protestant community best known to Englishmen.
Travellers in France of all classes generally stayed with Huguenot families, and carried letters of introduction to Huguenot
ministers, teachers, scholars and bankers. Intellectual communication with France was mainly with Huguenots and was disrupted by the Revocation, to be resumed mainly with those
who emigrated to Holland. There was some intermarriage.
Huguenots often acted as agents or factors for English merchants, and had lived in England. Of course it was precisely
these close links with foreign Protestants which angered Louis
and all zealous French Catholics; Huguenots really were
'separatists', more closely akin to the English and the Dutch
than to the majority of their own countrymen. In general the
Huguenot position was not unlike that of the English Catholics
in reverse, but with two differences; there were more of them,
nearly a million, and their rights were guaranteed by the Edict.
    There was a direct connection between the treatment of
religious minorities in the two countries. French attitudes
towards England were very largely coloured by religion.
Catholics had interpreted the execution of Charles I and the
rise of Cromwell as the inevitable consequences of Protestant
principles. The sufferings of the English and Irish Catholics
had always received much emphasis, and during the Popish
Plot great resentment had been provoked by the execution of
Jesuits and of Archbishop Plunket. Huguenots suffered from
this back-lash of resentment, but in fact pressure against them
had already begun to intensify, and had led to parliamentary
attacks against Catholicism during the mid-1670s. Religious
animosities in the two countries were inter-connected, but there
was a most striking difference in the effects of repression. In
Britain persecution was intermittently cruel, but social forces,
rather than direct pressure, were responsible for the gradual
erosion of the Catholic minority. In France similar social
pressures eliminated the Huguenot section of the nobility, but
left the bourgeois and peasant mass relatively untouched. Then,
within the four years 1682–86, ruthless repression overwhelmed
the Huguenots, driving the majority into conversion and a
minority into emigration. This swift and almost total oblitera-

tion of such a large and well-established religious minority contrasted with the survival of the Catholics in Britain, and was a testimony of the *power* of the French state as well as of the Catholic church. Moreover the techniques used in France might well be used in Britain by James, Father Petre, Melfort and other fanatics. James was already centralizing administration, enlarging the army with Catholics, using patronage to encourage conversions and attempting to give religious orders privileged positions in education. *Dragonnades*, the wholesale purchase of conversions, the exclusion of non-Catholics from government offices and the professions, the imprisonment of Protestant clergy, were all methods which had been used in Scotland with effect. And if it is objected that such methods could never have succeeded in England, there was every prospect of their doing so in predominantly Catholic Ireland.

Every section of the population was well informed of the persecution in France. Sermons accompanied the collections which almost every parish made for Huguenot relief. Refugees were widely dispersed. Attempts to suppress printed accounts, which culminated in the official burning of Claude's *Les Plaintes des Protestants cruellement opprimés dans le Royaume de France* served only to discredit James. Anglican clergy exhorted their congregations to prepare for tests of faith and endurance similar to those which the Huguenots were undergoing. Moreover English residents, and even tourists in France were directly affected by the Revocation. Dying Protestants were mercilessly harried by proseletyzing priests. The dead were refused burial rights, and several times the corpses of English men and women were exhumed, and dragged naked and decomposing through the streets of Paris. Official restrictions made travel increasingly unattractive. The France of Louis XIV, now at its most powerful, was forfeiting its cultural influence on England, every aspect of its civilization being suffused with the principles of arrogantly triumphant absolutism and militant Catholicism. This was not the France of the *salons*, of a tolerant, cynical and sophisticated society, a *douceur de vivre*, which eighteenth-century francophiles were to know, but a cruder France in which everything was subordinated to royal glory and power politics. The aspects of French life which James II's subjects saw were different from those regarded as significant by posterity – not Molière but Louvois, not the building of Versailles but the demolition of the *temple* at Charenton; the cruelty and the poverty, not the glory. When to this was added the effects of long wars and, after 1704, of almost continuous French defeats, it is not surprising that, apart from Jacobites, most Englishmen lost their former admiration for France.

The Revocation also destroyed the long-established Anglo-French communities in such ports as Nantes and Bordeaux. Pressure was exerted on Protestant residents to turn Catholic, some were imprisoned or deported, but more often their French-born wives and families were attacked. For these, and for those merchants and artisans who had become naturalized to help their business, the English envoys could do nothing, and they had the greatest difficulty in securing any relaxation of the laws for those who were undeniably British subjects. By the coming of war in 1689 formerly English and Protestant families were being rapidly assimilated.

Moderate Catholics in England had hoped to obtain a status of equality of civil rights and limited rights of worship similar to that of the Huguenots. A few priests had thought that part, at least, of the Anglican Church could be brought to accept Papal authority, provided that it retained privileges similar to those possessed by the Gallican Church. The torrent of hate created by the Revocation swept away these hopes. It hopelessly discredited James. Few would believe in his sincerity in advocating toleration, or in promising to respect the rights of the church. His extremist ministers, Father Petre and Melfort, were right when they advised him to strengthen his resolve. Unless he made full use of the army and the adminstration, incomparably weaker though it was than the French, to enforce his policies he must eventually submit to his subjects. But even in possession of the machinery of state, with Ireland controlled by Tyrconnel, James could have succeeded only with direct assistance from France. This Louis had neither the wish nor, after August 1688, the opportunity to provide. His attention was concentrated on Cologne and the Palatinate. As in 1679–81 he would be satisfied if British affairs were again plunged into prolonged confusion, as seemed likely to be the outcome when William launched his invasion.

CHAPTER SEVEN

The French Wars

THE accession of William and Mary in 1689 was automatically followed by British involvement in the general European war which had begun the previous autumn. This Nine Years War is often treated as a mere postscript to the 'Glorious Revolution', or as a preliminary to the victorious war of the Spanish Succession. In many ways the Nine Years War, through its effects, was as great a revolution as the actual constitutional changes. The long years of hard and at best inconclusive fighting placed a greater strain on Britain than it had ever experienced before. They were a national ordeal, a crucial test not just for the navy and the army, but also for Parliament and parliamentary methods of government, for the economy and for national unity and self-confidence.

In the first place this was a war of independence so far as England and Scotland were concerned. After 1688, and still more after the Boyne in 1690, James and the Jacobites were hopelessly and permanently compromised by their dependence on France and their association with militant Catholicism. The only realistic hope of a Restoration lay in a French conquest, as James recognized in his dying advice to his son: 'Be a good Catholic, fear God ... and after God be in an entire dependence on the King of France.' Secondly, this was the first major and prolonged war against France in modern times, the first of the series which continued until Waterloo. Statesmen, diplomats, admirals and generals now had to solve a new set of political and strategical problems with little experience to guide them. It is not surprising that William took on himself the virtual direction of both military and diplomatic affairs, that he preferred to use Dutch and Huguenot advisers and officers, or that so many disastrous mistakes were made, and wrong policies attempted, during the war. It is also important to realize how superior French resources were at this

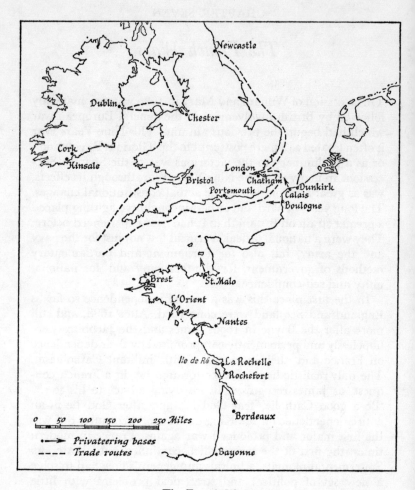

<figure>
Newcastle

Dublin

Chester

Cork

Kinsale

London

Bristol

Chatham

Portsmouth

Dunkirk

Calais

Boulogne

Brest

St. Malo

L'Orient

Nantes

Ile de Ré

La Rochelle

Rochefort

Bordeaux

Bayonne

0   50   100   150   200   250 Miles

•——→ Privateering bases
– – – Trade routes
</figure>

The French Wars

time; the population of France was more than three times that of the British Isles – and this included the disaffected Irish. The French armies consistently outnumbered their opponents, and in 1689 their fleet was larger than the British. The French economy could supply almost all the requirements of war, naval stores being the one important exception. Louis's proud motto, *Nec Pluribus Impar*, was valid; only a general coalition could check his power.

For Britain the struggle to avoid French domination involved membership, for the first time as a principal, in a wartime European alliance. Britain was assuming a diplomatic role which was to continue until the nineteenth century; a new and entirely unaccustomed role. Again, it is not surprising that inexperience and ignorance of European conditions led to serious errors being committed. Particular difficulties were involved in the arrangements for paying subsidies to allies and hiring mercenary contingents. Financial problems can be described as the most serious of all. Never before had Britain been engaged in such an expensive war, never had the economy come under such severe and prolonged strain through shipping losses, the disruption of foreign markets, bad harvests and unprecedentedly heavy war taxation. The avoidance of national bankruptcy, the establishment of the Bank of England and a national debt, the reform of the coinage and the financing of a vast programme of expenditure proved to a Europe over-impressed by French absolutism the relative efficiency and greater adaptability of the parliamentary system of government.

The geographical and strategic position of Britain in relation to France was in many ways difficult and unfavourable. Britain was the most vulnerable of all the allies to French attack. The French naval bases lay close to the main trade routes. An even greater danger was posed by the possibility of a French invasion which might, in one blow, destroy British independence. The prevention of such an invasion was the main task of the navy, but if French troops landed in any strength there was little to stop another 1066 or 1485; a campaign of a single decisive battle, followed by rapid submission. The Jacobites,

misled by specious promises, even hoped for a repetition of
1688, believing that the navy and army would refuse to resist a
major French attack. A French army would have faced only a
few, weak, regular units and the amateur militia; it might take
weeks to disengage and transport British and Dutch regiments
from Flanders to meet the invaders. Stiffened by French troops,
and supplied with arms, the Irish and Scottish Jacobites could
become formidable; the campaign in Ireland in 1689–91
weakened the allies in Flanders by diverting Dutch and Danish
as well as British troops, and by occupying William's attention.
French bases were strategically sited for launching invasions
of Ireland and Scotland; the Irish were supplied and equipped
from Brest and Nantes in 1689–91, and from Dunkirk the
Scottish east coast was vulnerable, as the expedition of 1708
showed. But a decisive invasion would have to be launched
across the Channel against southern England, and in this
area the French had to contend with serious difficulties, which
they never succeeded in overcoming. They had no large and
protected naval base between Brest and Dunkirk, whereas the
British fleet used Plymouth, the Downs and the virtually
invulnerable base of Portsmouth. The smaller French Channel
ports were ill-suited for the concentration of transports needed
for an invasion, while the main French fleet had limited sea-
keeping endurance. The large and heavily armed, but excessive-
ly crowded and unhygienic ships suffered appallingly from
disease, and many behaved badly in rough weather. These
defects, which forced Tourville to retire before he could effectively exploit his victory off Beachy Head in 1690, meant that
even if an army got ashore, its communications would soon be
left exposed to attack while the fleet withdrew to Brest for
victuals and repairs, and to land the sick. A British fleet in
being, as in 1690, could still obstruct French plans.

The defensive role of the navy, in preventing or deterring an
invasion, was often ignored by those who complained of the
cost of maintaining an apparently inactive main fleet – which
in fact did achieve very little after the victory of Barfleur in
1692. Its achievements as an instrument of the offensive were
necessarily limited. William made plans for a major invasion
of northern France to turn the enemy's left flank in Flanders,
but such an invasion never materialized, either in this or any

later French war. The bombardments of French ports did little damage. The attempted general blockade of France had negligible effects on the enemy war effort. William's one important contribution to the naval side of the war was to appreciate the influence which the British fleet could exert in the Mediterranean. Not only was it necessary to prevent the union of the Toulon with the Brest squadron, a major strategical problem in all the French wars, but the interests of our allies – Spain in 1689–97, the Emperor after 1701 – required protection. William feared that a French offensive into Catalonia would cause Spain, the weakest of all the allies, to make a separate peace. But if the British fleet was to afford effective protection on this front, by cutting French communications along the coast, it must winter in the Mediterranean, despite formidable difficulties of supply and refitting. This was in fact accomplished, using Cadiz, in 1694–95, and from this time, rather than from the earlier abortive occupation of Tangier, can be dated the British presence in the Mediterranean. After 1703 there was an additional commitment to protect Portugal and Portuguese trade with Brazil, and after 1704 Gibraltar had to be defended and supplied.

Disappointingly meagre results were produced by the other main offensive use of sea-power, the investment of men, ships and money in colonial campaigns, especially in the West Indies. Historians in the recent past, concerned to trace the origins and development of imperialist ideas and interests, tended to exaggerate the importance of colonial wars. Like seventeenth-century politicians they greatly underestimated the difficulties of conquering tropical territories. Disease, especially the yellow fever which was spreading epidemically at this time, wiped out unseasoned troops either in garrisons or when engaged in land fighting. Hurricanes and inadequate hydrographical information could lead to disastrous losses at sea. The plantations were not self-supporting in food, so that the maintenance of armies and fleets created serious administrative and logistical problems. Local authorities were notoriously self-interested and obstructive. The existence of these difficulties meant that little was achieved in attacking either the French islands in 1689–97, or the more extensive and apparently more vulnerable Spanish Empire after 1701. On the other hand

nothing was easier to organize and execute than colonial
raids, as the French showed in both wars. Expeditions on a
sufficiently large scale to overpower local defenses, plunder or
ransom a city and then withdraw, were a logical extension of
earlier buccaneering and privateering. Immense damage could
be done and large profits made. The element of surprise made
effective defence extremely difficult. Pointis took Cartagena in
1697, Duguay Trouin captured Rio in 1711, and British
ships and forts in West Africa were repeatedly and destructively raided, contributing to the collapse of the Royal African
Company.

Almost all naval historians have fallen into the Whig heresy
of interpreting the past in the light of current interests and
considerations. Believing in their own day that it was vital for
Britain to retain control of the seas by maintaining a fleet
equal in strength to that of all potential enemies combined,
they naturally argued that sea-power was, and always had
been, the decisive instrument of British policy. Certainly it is
true that control of the narrow seas was essential if invasion was
to be prevented and trade to continue, but both the Nine
Years War and the war of the Spanish Succession showed that
France could not be defeated, or even forced to concede a
satisfactory peace by the use of sea-power alone. French
strength was essentially land-based. Although Colbert had
expanded commerce and the colonies, it was not until at least
the war of 1744–48 that the French economy suffered significantly from British disruption of overseas and colonial
trade. On the other hand British trade, like that of the Dutch,
was vital to the economy and the war-effort, and also extremely vulnerable to attacks by the French privateers, the
guerre de course. British naval historians have always criticized
this French reliance on privateering, claiming that it could not
be decisive, that it diverted attention from the 'correct'
strategy which France 'ought' to have followed, of meeting
and beating the main British fleet, and so of 'winning' the
war.*

Now this interpretation may be valid for later Anglo-French

* This historical disparagement of the *guerre de course* probably contributed
to the belated realization of the importance of commerce protection in
1915–17.

wars, but Louis XIV did not expect to win a total victory in a
Napoleonic or modern sense; he lacked the power to conquer,
and the administrative capability to annex and absorb, his
enemies. It can be said that he aimed to 'dominate' his
neighbours, in the sense of being able to influence their
political and diplomatic decision-making so as to prevent them
following policies inimical to French interests. His strategy
was to exhaust his enemies so that they would agree to peace
on terms which would favour France, which would break up
the enemy coalition (as in 1678), and so give Louis the opportunity for a further round of territorial advances at the expense
of Spain. He placed as much reliance on diplomatic manoeuvres
during negotiations as on military victories, and in both the Nine
Years War and the War of the Spanish Succession his object
was to confirm and consolidate a highly favourable *status quo
ante bellum*. The only exception, the one possibility of a decisive
and final victory, lay in an invasion of England, which could
be consolidated by James's Restoration. Louis did not appreciate this possibility until it was too late. In 1689–90 he treated
Ireland as a sideshow. The French fleet was not used to disrupt
William's communications across the Irish Sea, no army was
ready to exploit Tourville's victory off Beachy Head in 1690;
failures which contrast with the bold and extremely successful
English combined operation against the Munster ports later
that year. In 1692, when serious preparations were made
for an invasion, inflexible orders from Louis led Tourville to
the disaster of Barfleur–La Hougue. After this, apart from the
scheme of 1696 which depended on William's murder and a
Jacobite rising, Louis reverted to the war of military attrition,
supplemented by diplomatic manoeuvres and intervention in
the politics of the United Provinces.

In a memorandum of 1695, when most of the main French
fleet had been laid up and the campaigns in Flanders had
become a stalemate, Vauban argued that only the *guerre de
course* could force Britain and the United Provinces to make
peace. By destroying their trade 'le nerf de la guerre' would
be cut. William would be unable to finance his allies, and
would come under pressure from mercantile interests to stop
the war. It can be argued that the *guerre de course* accomplished
this; shipping and trade losses made opinion in both countries

eager for peace in 1696–97, and in 1710–12 mercantile (as distinct from financial) interests favoured the Tory policy of peace. The Dutch attempt to continue the war in 1712–13 without England was undermined by catastrophic losses at sea.

In the privateering war France enjoyed the same advantage in relation to Britain, as we had earlier possessed over the Dutch. Brest and St. Malo were dangerously close to the Soundings, the focal area of the south-west approaches through which all trade with southern Europe, Asia, Africa and America passed. From Dunkirk all the North Sea routes were threatened. At this time warships could not keep the sea in all weathers, so that blockades of Brest could never be effective, while local knowledge of the shoals enabled privateers to get in and out of Dunkirk almost at will. French shipping offered a far smaller target; it was now the turn of such famous corsairs as Jean Bart, Duguay Trouin and Forbin to attack a 'mountain of gold'.* This *guerre de course* cost Louis little. Most commerce raiders were equipped by private interests, the *armateurs*, and royal ships employed after the main fleet was laid up could usually earn their own keep. Prize-money was an incentive to efficiency and enterprise. The French had already gained experience during the Dutch war of 1672–78, and after 1689 they were generally one move ahead of the allies' protective measures. As well as innumerable individual raiders, wolf-packs were operated against convoys, frigates attacking and often overwhelming the escort while smaller ships boarded the merchantmen. There was at this time no way of fixing a ship's longitude, and methods of estimating its latitudes were inaccurate, so that homeward-bound shipping tended to be so widely dispersed in the Soundings that effective protection was difficult to organize. When cruisers did begin to operate, the privateers switched their attack to other focal areas – the approaches to Lisbon and the Straits, the Skaggerak, and the Mediterranean narrows.

Trade losses reached almost intolerable levels during the Nine Years War, with a staggering total of around 4,000 ships captured or ransomed, mostly in the years 1693–97. The most spectacular French success was the partial destruction of the

* See above, p. 51.

joint English and Dutch Smyrna fleet off Lagos in 1693. Losses in 1702–13 were almost as heavy and may have been as many as 3,250. These casualties, together with the complete stoppage of Mediterranean trade in 1690–93, the long and frequent delays while convoys waited for escort, the increased insurance premiums and losses of cargoes in Dutch and neutral ships all threw an intense strain on the economy. Little compensation was gained from offensive action against France. In 1689–97 some 1,200 ships were taken, but a great deal of French trade continued, carried by Dutch ships. Despite the treaty of August 1689, prohibiting the practice, Dutch ships carried French exports and imports under licence from Louis, whereas all English trade with France was banned by statute. Understandably most Englishmen failed to realize how far Dutch trade with the Baltic depended on a continued supply of French goods, and complained that we were being exploited by rapacious allies. The attempt by Britain to stop French trade also raised questions of the right of search, of ownership and of what constituted contraband, which created difficulties with neutrals, despite agreements with Denmark in 1691 and Sweden in 1693.

On land, as at sea, the Nine Years War proved to be expensive, difficult and unsuccessful, yet it may be said that the British army first became important during William's reign. The army which William inherited was largely James II's creation; from 9,215 men in 1684 he had expanded its strength to 34,592 in 1687, and he had introduced reforms on the French model. The Ordnance had been organized, Quarter-Master-Generals established, systematic drill and Divisional and Brigade exercises instituted, and the proportion of cavalry to foot increased. Nevertheless this army was in many ways a liability. Apart from garrison service in Tangier it had no experience of war and, as its failure to oppose William had shown, many units were soft from prolonged inactivity in camps placed, for political reasons, too near London. Regiments with a high proportion of Irish and Scottish Catholics were politically disaffected. All units were weakened by the replacement of politically suspect officers by strangers. The winter camp at Dundalk in 1689–90 revealed the most appalling defects of administration, field organization and regimental care; 6,300 soldiers died out of a total strength of 14,000. The lack of experienced officers was reflected in the preponderance of Dutchmen, Germans and Huguenots in commands, but William seems consistently and wrongly to have undervalued British officers – the most obvious example being his suspension of Marlborough. The lack of a military tradition can also be seen in the attitude of public and parliamentary opinion. Recruits had to be obtained through crimps, by allowing imprisoned debtors their freedom if they enlisted and, in Scotland, by annual impressment. Parliamentary debates reveal a continued fear of standing armies and little understanding of military affairs. Criticisms were often based on irrelevant examples from the past, for instance that if Cromwell had needed only 16,000 men to conquer Ireland, why should William require over 35,000? From the start many members argued that Britain should not take a major part in the continental fighting; her contribution should be limited to the 10,000 men stipulated in the Dutch treaty of 1678. This same assumption lay beneath the apparently suicidal insistence on disbanding the bulk of the army in 1697–98. A reduction to 7,000 men on the English establishment, and 12,000 on the Irish, was intended to prevent Britain's being 'exploited' again for the benefit of the allies. Even stronger criticisms were directed against the maintenance of foreign troops at our expense, a theme which was to be repeated throughout the eighteenth century.

The continental campaigns were also criticized, more realistically, on strategic grounds: whether it was wise to concentrate such a high proportion of our limited resources against the French in Flanders, the area where they were strongest. The fighting there proved to be a bloody ordeal for the regiments engaged, this being the aspect of the war which military historians have examined in detail. The more general question of military organization still requires further research. Treatment on a comparative basis with the Dutch and French services might be productive, and an assessment is needed of the effects of the military war-effort, fiscally and administratively, on the government as a whole. Recent work on the administration of the navy has thrown light on the way in which Parliament became directly concerned with the problems created by the complexity and magnitude of the war at sea. This raises several important questions. It has been argued that the structure of the British economy was such that it naturally supported, as well as required, the maintenance of a large and efficient navy, but that this was not so in the case of France. This suggests the examination of a parallel hypothesis; that the existence of the British, but not the French, army was less natural and its maintenance more difficult, and that this can be seen in the disbanding of most of the army in 1697–98, and again in the eagerness to disengage and demobilize after 1710. Again there is an important difference between the two services in that money spent on the navy was largely expended in Britain, on victuals, shipbuilding and maintenance, dockyard work and wages paid to crews on discharge; while army expenditure was mostly made abroad. This meant not only a charge on the balance of payments but also easy opportunities for major frauds on the part of agents, paymasters and contractors. Shipping and shipbuilding, important industrial interests, were directly stimulated by the war, whereas the land war was fought in theatres which although strategically vital were of lesser economic value. The navy, apart from a declining Dutch contribution, fought alone, but the army included large foreign contingents and involved the administration in complicated arrangements with foreign governments and generals. Parliament knew less, and cared less for the novel and potentially dangerous army and its operations than for the navy.

Parliamentary interest in the navy was not always or necessarily an advantage. The Admiralty commission of M.P.s appointed in 1679 had proved to be incompetent and factious. A majority of members still instinctively distrusted and opposed the executive, and while unsparing in criticism the Commons were reluctant to accept responsibility. When, after long and bitter criticisms of maladministration of the army in Ireland, William replied by asking the Commons to superintend preparations for the campaign of 1690, they declined. The first parliamentary commissioners for auditing public accounts (1691) behaved as Opposition politicians. Some of their positive proposals were impracticable and would have undermined the authority of the executive; for instance, the stipulation in the 1694 Land Tax of the number of cruisers to be equipped for commerce protection, and the 1695 project for a Council of Trade, nominated by Parliament, which could act independently of the Admiralty in matters of commerce protection. Parliament was slow to realize that its deliberate failure to vote William and Mary the former hereditary revenues, for obvious political reasons, entailed assuming administrative responsibilities, but its contribution to the waging of the war was crucial. As in the Dutch wars finance was as important as the fighting, but this time it was the enemy, the French, who were weakened by fiscal and administrative defects, a declining economy and eventually virtual bankruptcy.

There is room in this study for only one aspect of this subject to be examined. The fiscal innovations which the wars necessitated, especially the excises and the land taxes, were often denounced, as 'Dutch finance'. This can be interpreted as meaning that the new taxes were imitations of Dutch ones, that Britain was coming to rival the Dutch as the most heavily taxed nation in Europe, and that the Dutch, especially by investing in the Bank of England, were direct beneficiaries. These assertions should not be taken very seriously; the Dutch were still natural scapegoats. Throughout the century Englishmen had been constantly exhorted to imitate the Dutch as the surest and quickest way to economic prosperity, and Downing and Clifford, both deadly enemies of the Dutch, had advocated fiscal reforms on the Dutch model: lower customs, fewer duties on exports but a wide extension of excises. But abstract exhortations had had little effect. Only after 1688, with the desperate need to finance the war and avoid national bankruptcy, were fundamental changes and developments undertaken. And although some of these may appear to be imitations of Dutch models, this was not the case. The Bank of England was established, to play an indispensable part in establishing national credit and financing the army in Flanders. In turn it could not have survived without an improvement in the efficiency of revenue collection, and here the key to solvency can be found in the extended use of excises. Superficially the Bank of England may resemble the Bank of Amsterdam, and contemporaries linked excises with Holland. But there were differences more important than these resemblances. After 1683 the excises were not farmed – as was still the case in the eighteenth-century United Provinces. Proposals in 1700 for the revival of farming were rejected, and it has been argued that the appointment of revenue officials on the basis of their efficiency, and an apprenticeship, marks the first important change from the earlier proprietorial attitude to office holding which England had had in common with many European countries.* The relationship between the executive and Parliament was as unique in the financial as in the constitutional fields. If any source of inspiration or example is to be found for the principle of appropriation, the practice of parliamentary estimates and auditing, the securing of loans on parliamentary guarantees of repayment, it is to be found in the administration of the Long Parliament and the Commonwealth, not in contemporary Holland.

The most obvious point which any comparison of the conduct of the Nine Years War with that of the War of the Spanish Succession brings out is the contrast between William's military failures and Marlborough's great victories. William allowed himself to be outmanoeuvred strategically and tactically, and he always suffered from a serious inferiority in numbers. As in 1672–78 his battles, Steenkirk and Landen, were near-disasters; his one major success a siege, that of Namur. He barely succeeded in preventing the French from overrunning the Spanish Netherlands, and if by his dogged resistance he reduced both the morale and the striking power of France in a war of attrition, he was also exhausting Britain and the United Provinces. The military problems which Marlborough faced were initially far greater. With French troops in occupation of the Spanish Netherlands, the Dutch were pinned back in defence of their own frontiers, a precarious position which accounts for their military caution, which all British historians have rather sweepingly condemned. Marlborough's primary task was to eject the numerically

* See E. Hughes, *Studies in Administration and Finance* (1934), Chapter V.

superior French forces from the most highly fortified region in Europe, and not until the campaign of 1709 did he have an advantage in numbers. Moreover the French army was reasonably homogeneous, while Marlborough's was a mixture of British, Dutch, Danes, Germans, Huguenots and others. The French generals were usually hampered by Louis, who attempted to control operations from Versailles; Marlborough found the Dutch field-deputies an equally vexatious restriction on his freedom. Like William, Marlborough was distracted by political differences and parliamentary difficulties which frequently necessitated his presence in England, and he too had also to keep an eye on the affairs of all Europe; for instance, in 1707 he had to travel to Altranstadt to persuade Charles XII of Sweden not to attack Austria. William had the sickeningly difficult task of holding together an unsuccessful coalition; Marlborough faced the more subtle problems of preventing his allies from indulging in the luxury of quarrels once Louis need no longer be feared militarily. His diplomatic problems increased in complexity and gravity almost in proportion to his military successes as a general.*

Marlborough's masterpiece, the victory of Blenheim, deserved all the praise lavished on it. In 1704 there was a real danger of the French offensive, with Bavarian co-operation, forcing the Emperor to make peace. The march to the Danube involved enormous risks and difficulties. In its daring, skilful organization and swift execution only one operation can be compared with it – William's invasion of England in 1688, the most underestimated military enterprise of the whole period. The difference was that Blenheim represented a victory over the French army, Louis's main instrument of power, and that it was followed by further offensive successes. Ramillies (1706) and Oudenarde (1708) at long last secured the Low Countries from French expansionist ambitions, and destroyed the margin of military superiority which Louis had depended upon. The capture in 1708 of Lille, the strongest of the frontier fortresses, put the French permanently on the defensive. Yet,

---

* A fascinating study could be made of the relation between Churchill's analysis of Marlborough's career and his own later conduct of the Second World War; it is significant that after the decisive battles had been won, Kursk and Tunis in 1943, the anti-Nazi coalition began to fall apart.

in their consequences, the defects of Marlborough's character proved to be more important than William's lack of comparable military genius. William's fatalism, endurance and obstinacy equipped him for his lifelong mission of checking French expansion, however adverse the circumstances, as in 1672. But his hostility to Louis did not prevent him from negotiating a compromise peace at Ryswick in 1697 and the two Partition treaties, in the attempt to avoid the disaster of another ruinous European war. On the other hand, Marlborough did not take advantage of his victories to make peace in 1709–10 on highly advantageous terms. Over-confidence, self-interest and cupidity led him to fall in with the Whig policy of 'no peace without Spain', a continuation of the war until Louis was crushed and forced to capitulate.

This Whig policy of forcing Louis to abandon his grandson Philip, or even to drive him from the throne, depended on Marlborough's victories rather than on allied strength and achievements in Spain itself. The fact that a campaign in Spain could be attempted at all was due to British naval superiority. Starting with a badly organized and feebly executed attempt on Cadiz in 1702, whose failure was concealed by the spectacular destruction of the Treasure fleet in Vigo, Gibraltar was seized in 1704 and subsequently held and supplied, a much harder task. The one fleet action of the war, off Malaga (August 1704), ended indecisively but the damage to the French fleet was never fully repaired, and most of its ships were subsequently scuttled in Toulon, leaving the British in full control of the Mediterranean. Supported and supplied from the sea, small allied forces were able to raise rebellions and establish themselves in Catalonia and Valencia, but attempts to invade and subdue Castile ended in failures; defeat at Almanza in 1707 and at Brihuega in 1710.

These defeats in Spain, together with the relative success of the French defensive strategy in 1709–11, meant that a decision could not be reached by military means. In 1709 the 'victory' of Malplaquet cost appalling losses. These three years' campaigns were occupied with slow sieges, expensive in men and money, and masterly manoeuvres which forced the French out of one line of fortifications only for Marlborough to be faced with another. To quote a contemporary critic, 'A town in a

year will not make the war cease'. The expenditure which
these wars entailed, the losses of merchant ships at sea and,
above all, Whig exploitation of the war for their own political
advantage, created a general revulsion against the war, whose
most obvious manifestation was ill-feeling against the allies in
general, and the Dutch in particular.

At the ministerial level, in diplomatic terms, relations with
the Emperor were the most troublesome. His reluctance to use
titles which implied the legitimacy of Queen Anne's sovereignty
contrasted with the ill-requited efforts made by British fleets
and armies on behalf of the Archduke Charles, the Habsburg
claimant to the Spanish succession. British troops carried the
load of the Spanish campaigns, while the Emperor concentrated on the territories in Italy which were his real objective.
His conquests, Naples, Sicily and Sardinia, could not have
been made without the British navy. Austria consolidated
these gains in the most selfish way, by concluding an armistice
which permitted Louis to evacuate his troops and transfer them
to oppose the allies in Spain. In the Spanish Netherlands the
Emperor tried to gain his rights by the equally short-sighted
tactic of creating suspicion and ill-will between the English and
the Dutch, for instance by the offer of the Governorship to
Marlborough. For those who saw the war as a struggle against
absolutism and persecuting Catholicism, Imperial methods
were as objectionable as those employed by Louis. In Hungary
the systematic subversion of aristocratic constitutional liberties
was combined with harsh repression of Protestantism. Moreover the practical consequences materially weakened the
allies; Hungarian rebellions diverted Imperial troops from the
weak Rhine front.

The Whigs were outraged by Imperial policy in Hungary,
but the public in general remained largely indifferent. In
contrast, although real grievances against the Dutch were less
serious and less well founded, they were eagerly accepted by
much of the nation and easily exploited by Tory politicians
and propagandists. The way was prepared by the earlier
outburst of 1697–1700, when it had been alleged that England
was governed by Dutchmen for the benefit of the United
Provinces. Born in war-weariness, fed by the belief that the
Dutch profited from war at our expense, a general hostility to

them became as important a factor in domestic politics as the unpopularity of Whig religious policy. Tory writers like Swift, by appealing to this hostility, were able to convince public opinion that a continuation of the war was both unnecessary and damaging to British interests. Passing quickly over the origins of the war, ignoring the series of provocations which Louis had committed in 1700–01 *after* his acceptance of Carlos II's will – his occupation of the Spanish Netherlands, the trade embargo on British ships, his plans for commercial penetration of the Spanish Empire in America, and his recognition of James III – the Tories implied that the war had from the first been for the benefit of the English ministers and their Dutch associates.

For as long as France remained a military and political threat, down to 1708, it is surprising how little criticism was directed against the Dutch. Marlborough rarely expressed his resentment at Dutch restrictions. Dutch failures to pay agreed subsidies to allies, to set out their quota of ships, their continued trade with France, the disputes over administration and trade in the conquered Spanish Netherlands and over the disposal of English ships taken by the French and recaptured by Zeeland privateers, all remained minor irritants. The English ministers did not make an issue out of them for fear that the Dutch might succumb to a French peace offensive. The Dutch were the weak link in the alliance, and the most likely to make a separate peace. Louis recognized this by concentrating his propaganda and diplomatic approaches on them. This would have left Britain, like the Confederates in 1678, to negotiate singly with France. In such circumstances there would have been no chance of obtaining one of the main objectives of a satisfactory peace, recognition of the Protestant succession by Louis. In the years of tension before the Union treaty with Scotland this was a matter of urgency, and the ministry in 1708–09 were ready to make concessions to the Dutch in return for their guarantee of the Act of Settlement. This is what Townshend obtained in the Barrier treaty of 1709; his critics alleged that he paid the Dutch an excessive price, giving them virtual domination over the Spanish Netherlands, and sacrificing trading interests by promising equal opportunities to the Dutch in Spanish America.

The offers of peace which Louis made to the Dutch had ulterior purposes. Certainly France needed peace by 1709, but as in 1676–78 Louis hoped to split the allies, who cannot be blamed for distrusting his approaches. It is easy for the historian to exaggerate the effects of Marlborough's victories on French power, and to underestimate the resilience and skill of its military and diplomatic systems. The allied demand which Louis rejected, in article 37 of the preliminary articles of May 1709, that France must secure Philip V's withdrawal from Spain – by force if necessary – was not so unreasonable as is usually supposed. If a truce was made leaving Philip defiantly in possession of Spain, the allies would be committed to a difficult war, while France had time to recover. If an armistice was concluded in Flanders it was doubtful if the Dutch would resume hostilities. This was the Whig justification for making concessions to the Dutch in the Barrier treaty, and they were repaid when the latter rejected French offers at the Gertruydenberg negotiations in 1710. The Dutch were now tied to the Whig line of no peace without Spain, but this policy went far beyond actual British interests. It afforded the prospect of apparently perpetual war and an equally perpetual Whig ministry, a war in which there were obvious advantages for the Whigs and their associates, but no corresponding gains for the nation.

The war, its conduct and the taxation which it required, provided some of the principal political issues throughout the reign of Queen Anne. It did not directly cause the ministerial changes which began in 1710 and converted a Whig dominated ministry into a predominantly Tory one, but the subsequent rout of Whigs in the general election of 1710 was due to their identification with the war as well as with the Sacheverel impeachment. This fact committed the new ministers to the early conclusion of a satisfactory peace with France, and in their view this meant satisfying specifically British demands and interests, with little regard for those of the allies. Harley and St. John kept the Dutch under pressure, complaining at each failure to meet their obligations. Starting with the unofficial approach through Gaultier in the winter of 1710–11, they negotiated secretly for an agreement with France without consulting the Dutch or considering their interests. The

Preliminaries agreed on with France in October 1711 virtually predetermined the issues at the Utrecht conference which opened in January 1712. The Barrier treaty was repudiated in February, demonstrating in practice the principle of disregard for the allies which St. John expressed; 'Britain has gone much too far in weaving her interest with that of the Continent . . . it will prove no easy task to disentangle our affairs without tearing or rending.'

The propaganda by which the Tory ministry justified their policy of national selfishness appealed to popular xenophobia with great effect, but a more reasoned political argument was the intimate and continuing association of the allies with the fallen Whigs. It should be remembered that the full title of Swift's famous pamphlet was, *The Conduct of the Allies and of the Late Ministry in Beginning and Carrying on the Present War.* The repeated attempts by allied ambassadors to excite public opinion against the peace merely confirmed Tory propaganda, that the allies were still trying to exploit Britain and that the Whigs would sacrifice national interests in order to recover office and power. Another principal Tory argument was to emphasize the cost of the war, and the unequal burdens which it imposed. They appealed to the masses, whose living standards had been reduced by the extension of excises, to the country gentlemen and farmers who paid the bulk of the Land Tax, and to the merchants who were suffering heavily at sea. Their sacrifices were contrasted with the allegedly enormous profits being made by the 'Monied Men', the financial interests, out of the war. There were other reasons why this section should be hated; their wealth largely escaped taxation, many of its members were foreigners of Dutch origin who retained their Amsterdam connections, and some were Jews or dissenters – who were equally detested by both High Tories and the urban masses. Similarly and more justifiably unpopular were the lesser branches of the financial world, government contractors, stock jobbers and speculators.

Tory attacks on those financial interests that had been associated with the war and the Whigs were accompanied by an attempt to secure the support of the main commercial and trading interests. This is a subject which requires further investigation, but it seems to have been entirely tactical and opportunist; Bolingbroke in particular wanted their support for short-term political purposes but had little idea of the real needs of British commerce, and little patience in overcoming difficulties. The treaty of Utrecht itself did secure some basic British interests. Bolingbroke appreciated the importance of retaining bases for the protection of Mediterranean trade, remembering the outcry of 1700 against William's concession of Naples and Sicily to France in the second Partition treaty. He insisted on Gibraltar and Minorca. France had to recognize the British position in Acadia, Hudson's Bay and Newfoundland, although slovenly drafting of the clauses on French rights in Newfoundland fishing waters and coasts caused two centuries of difficulties. The ministry was pledged to gain satisfaction for the South Sea Company, founded under Tory auspices in 1711 as a means of financing the last stages of the war independently of the Whig-associated financial interests. Its major objective was apparently achieved in March 1713 with the Spanish concession of the *Asiento*, the importation of Negro slaves into the Spanish American colonies. This was followed in July by a satisfactory preliminary commercial treaty concerning trade with Spain itself. But the *Asiento* soon proved to be unsatisfactory in important details, and the final commercial treaty of 1713 a disaster, partly because of diplomatic carelessness and also as a result of Spanish bribes to the commissioner of trade, Arthur Moore, and probably to Bolingbroke himself.

Most historians have approved of the treaty of Utrecht, both as a satisfactory European settlement and in furthering British interests. In detail many sectional interests were extremely dissatisfied at the time; in particular the commercial clauses which would have abolished most of the restrictions on trade with France were narrowly defeated in the Commons. In the long run the treaty of Utrecht succeeded because it embodied an existing and durable balance of power in Europe, but for the overwhelming majority of the nation the conclusion of peace after more than two decades of war was all that mattered.

CHAPTER EIGHT

Conclusion

IN surveying the period as a whole there is a clear contrast between Britain's comparative isolation and unimportance in European affairs at the beginning of the seventeenth century, and her full involvement as a major influence after 1688. This is as true in intellectual as in political matters. Intellectual influences are, by their nature, difficult to trace and substantiate. In individual cases it is possible to estimate the importance of travel or education abroad in a man's intellectual development (for instance, Hobbes's periods of residence in France and Inigo Jones's Italian travels), and of meetings and correspondence between scholars and academies or societies. But it would be accurate to say that, in general, European intellectual developments during the first part of the century did not significantly affect the main currents of English life, and that English influences on Europe (apart from the United Provinces) were negligible. It is significant that the only groups interested in, and connected with, developments in Europe were those minorities who were dissatisfied with the established order in Britain. For most of those who can be described as 'Puritans' the Calvinist churches of Europe provided the model which they hoped to establish in England. During James I's reign they were directly inspired by Dutch divines, universities and controversies, and encouraged in their opposition to royal and episcopal policies by the decrees of the synod of Dort. In intellectual as in economic matters Scotland was virtually a colony of Holland. But the partly formed Calvinist international, to which English Puritans and Scottish Presbyterians belonged, together with German, Czech, Swiss, Magyar, French and Dutch churches, did not survive the 1620s. It was shattered in the early disastrous phases of the Thirty Years War, and by the submission of the Huguenots (when Louis XIII insisted on the elimination of foreign pastors), so that by the time that English Puritanism temporarily triumphed during the abortive English Revolution it retained few European connections of any importance, and was dependent on its own intellectual resources, supplemented by those of Scotland and New England – a very different position from that of the Reformers a century before.

The connections which bound militant Catholicism with Europe were more durable. Isolated and often under pressure at home, English Catholics regarded themselves as part of the community of Christendom and as following the tradition of the past, from which their fellow-countrymen had been severed by the arbitrary decisions of Henry VIII and Elizabeth. Before 1640 it was the religious doctrines, rituals and claims to universality of Catholicism that attracted converts, but after 1660 it was the political rather than the religious aspects of Catholicism which attracted those court circles which admired and wished to imitate the France of Louis XIV. The prestige of French culture, imbued as so much of it was with Catholic principles and beliefs, and the power and glory of the French monarchy reinforced the purely religious appeal of Catholicism to the upper classes. The defeat of Catholicism, inextricably connected as it was in the minds of contemporaries with absolutism and Louis XIV, is the main theme of English history in the late seventeenth century, while the events of 1686–90 renewed and strengthened the links between Catholicism and the Irish national spirit.

The end of isolation was a very gradual process. The most important factor before 1688 was the diversification, as well as expansion, of overseas trade, in both exports and imports. Instead of trade being confined largely to a few traditional staple products, and following routes and patterns going back to medieval times, the new trades which were developed – the European being at first far more important than the oriental and colonial – assumed greater economic importance. A study of the relations of Britain with each European country that was open to maritime trade, for which there is unfortunately no space in this survey, would show how closer economic ties inevitably produced political connections years before Britain became fully and permanently involved in the European diplomatic system. For example, Britain had to become a

Mediterranean power and began to intervene in Portuguese politics during Charles II's reign. In addition, foreign travel on an expanded scale widened the outlook of the educated, and there appears to have been a more extensive knowledge of foreign languages, particularly French. But it must be stressed that, apart from this economic impact, England made little impression on Europe before 1688. There was almost universal ignorance of the English language, so that English literature was hardly known to exist. The political instability and continual violence of British affairs bewildered or horrified all Europeans except the Dutch, so that to them the issues at stake were unintelligible. Again only the Dutch had any realization of actual or potential English power. It was only after 1688 that Britain became fully and irrevocably involved in European affairs, so that even if, as the Whig historians claimed, the Revolution involved no essential break in constitutional continuity, it must be emphasized that it entirely transformed Britain's relationship with Europe.

The two wars which followed the Revolution affected the lives of every inhabitant of the British Isles in a way which the political changes did not. They involved major changes, which were usually uncomfortable and often disastrous, to individuals and economic interests. All sections of the population, every part of the administration, came under intense and prolonged strain, and it is not surprising that (as the political debates of 1697–1701 showed) there was widespread and bitter resentment. Foreign trade and shipping suffered exceptionally severely. But while individuals went under, the nation not only survived its ordeal but became stronger – administratively, politically and economically as well as militarily. Parliamentary government proved itself. A mood of national confidence developed out of the ordeals of William's war and Marlborough's victories.

The effects of these wars on the United Provinces were very different. The strain was more than their resources and national morale could bear, and it had more than purely material consequences. After a period of cultural primacy the Dutch became mere intermediaries, contributing little of their own, while the upper classes succumbed to an indiscriminate francomania. Much more revealing and significant is a comparison with France. The strains involved by the wars on

Britain and France were comparable, for if Louis had to fight against most of Europe his country was already organized for war, whereas Britain was not. The fact that the French economy was relatively undeveloped offset the advantages of a much larger population, an absolutist political system and a central geographical position, but it also meant that France could not be brought to the point of collapse as Britain and the United Provinces would have been had the *guerre de course* succeeded. Despite bankruptcy and successive defeats Louis could repeatedly raise new armies from the peasant masses, and prolong resistance indefinitely – at the cost of appalling popular suffering, which reached unendurable levels in 1693–95 and 1709–10. But, as the research of modern French social historians has shown, the French peasant was accustomed to living on, or below, the subsistence level. All the achievements and splendour of the *grand siècle*, its culture and art, Versailles, the *noblesse de robe* as much as the old aristocracy, the Church, to a large extent the towns and Louis's foreign policy, were all based on a mass of peasant-pauper misery such as did not exist in England – although it did in Ireland, where it had to support a similar social and military superstructure. After 1678 the French peasantry were too suppressed to try to renew on a large scale the bloody but unsuccessful risings which Richelieu's wars had provoked. Nevertheless the sufferings of the people, and the lack of even compensatory victories and territorial advances after 1688, discredited the *ancien régime* in a more indirect way. The thesis has been developed by Paul Hazard and Professor Mousnier that the classical emphasis on order and form, on discipline and certainty, was an attempt to preserve an established order and orthodoxy which was beginning to crumble.* Although the contemporary critics were few and relatively restrained and the reaction after 1715 largely trivial and ephemeral, Louis's reign ended in political and intellectual as well as financial bankruptcy.

It would be difficult to demonstrate any direct connection between the development of British power and economic expansion, and the advances in philosophy, mathematics and

---

* R. Mousnier, *Les XVIe et XVIIe siècles. Histoire générale des civilisations*, IV (3rd edition, 1961).

P. Hazard, *The European Mind, 1680–1715* (Pelican Edition, 1964).

science which made such a profound impression on European
intellectuals in the early eighteenth century. Most of the scholars and scientists concerned were more than normally insulated
from the politics of the world in which they lived – this was
true of Newton, Boyle, Ray and Flamsteed, to mention only
four. Most, but not all, of the scientists and philosophers of the
late seventeenth century were convinced believers in the
truth of revealed religion, and made strenuous efforts to
demonstrate that the new discoveries actually strengthened,
not subverted, Christianity. Today we may regard their
reconciliation of the new science with old revelation as
facile and theoretically unsatisfactory. But the point to be
emphasized is that neither they, *nor any large section of educated
opinion* in Britain at this time, consciously desired to use new
ideas for an offensive against religion, whereas in France
Bayle's *Dictionary* was to be used to mount all-out attacks and
these were soon to lead to the alienation from Christianity of a
large proportion of the educated classes. The Latitudinarians
who William appointed, by their emphasis on tolerance and
rational religion, played a vital role in preventing, or at least
postponing, the formation of an influential group of enemies of
religion in England. Admittedly the latitudinariarian Stilling-
fleet attacked Locke, and it may only have been Locke's
personal timidity which prevented him from pushing his ideas
to their logical conclusion, but there was no repetition of the
earlier and frenzied 'hunting of Leviathan'. Hobbes's writings
had been as subversive of the political constitution as of
religion, whereas Locke's *Two Treatises of Government* gave theo-
retical justification to the Revolution. Moreover, when Hobbes
wrote there had been physical, material, social and spiritual
confusion and uncertainty; after 1688 England could at last
feel relatively secure and English opinion was generally
satisfied with the political and social order.

It was this sense of security, of insular confidence, and
their accompaniments of military power and upper-class and
bourgeois affluence which impressed contemporary Europe. In
addition, due largely to Huguenot exiles who acted as trans-
lators and disseminators of English science, theology and
philosophy, Europeans were also made to realize that England
possessed an autonomous culture.

Further Reading

General
R. Davis, *The Rise of the English Shipping Industry* (1962).
M. Lewis, *The History of the British Navy* (1957).
A. T. Mahan, *The Influence of Sea Power upon History* (1890).
C. Wilson, *England's Apprenticeship* (1965).
A. Browning (Ed.), *English Historical Documents*, Vol. VIII (1660–1714), Part X.

Chapter 1
J. W. Stoye, *English Travellers Abroad, 1604–1667* (1952).
F. N. L. Poynter (Ed.), James Yonge, *The Journal* (1963). A vivid account of life at sea.

Chapter 2
C. H. Carter, *The Secret Diplomacy of the Habsburgs* (1964). 'Gondomar: Ambassador to James I', *Historical Journal*, VI, 2 (1964).
R. Davis, 'England and the Mediterranean, 1570–1670', in Ed. F. J. Fisher, *Essays in the Economic and Social History of Tudor and Stuart England* (1961).
A. Friis, *Alderman Cockayne's Project and the Cloth Trade* (1927).
R. W. K. Hinton, *The Eastland Trade and the Common Weal* (1957).
A. P. Newton, *The Colonizing Activities of the English Puritans* (New Haven, 1914).
B. Supple, *Commercial Crisis and Change in England, 1600–42* (1959).
R. H. Tawney, *Business and Politics under James I* (1958).

Chapter 3
G. Ascoli, *La Grande Bretagne devant l'opinion française* (Paris, 1930).
M. P. Ashley, *Financial and Commercial Policy under the Protectorate* (1962).
T. Aston (Ed.), *Crisis in Europe, 1650–1660* (1965). This consists of essays and discussions which have appeared in *Past and Present*.
D. A. Bigby, *Anglo-French Relations, 1641 to 1649* (1933).
C. Hill, *Puritanism and Revolution* (1962).
M. Prestwich, 'Diplomacy and Trade in the Protectorate', *Journal of Modern History*, XXII, 2 (1950).

For Marxist interpretations see,
M. H. Dobb, *Studies in the Development of Capitalism* (1946).
C. Hill, 'Soviet Interpretations of the English Interregnum', *Economic History Review*, 1st series, VIII, 2 (1938).
A. L. Morton, *A People's History of England* (1938).

Chapters 4 and 5
C. R. Boxer, *The Dutch Seaborne Empire* (1965).
K. G. Davies, *The Royal African Company* (1957).
G. Edmundson, *Anglo-Dutch Rivalry* (1911).
P. Geyl, *History of the Low Countries, Episodes and Problems* (1964).
    The Netherlands in the Seventeenth Century, Part 1 (1961), Part 2 (1964).
K. H. D. Haley, *William of Orange and the English Opposition* (1953).
D. Ogg, *England in the Reign of Charles II* (1955).
G. J. Renier, *The Dutch Nation* (1944).
B. H. M. Vlekke, *Evolution of the Dutch Nation* (New York, 1945).
C. Wilson, *Holland and Britain* (1945).
    Profit and Power (1957).

Documents
Sir G. Clark (Ed.), Sir William Temple, *Observations upon the United Provinces of the Netherlands* (1932).
S. R. Gardiner and C. T. Atkinson (Eds.), *Letters and Papers Relating to the First Dutch War, 1652–1654* (Navy Records Society, 6 Volumes, 1899–1930).
Thomas Mun, *England's Treasure by Fforraign Trade* (Reprint, Blackwell, Oxford, 1959).

Chapters 6 and 7
J. S. Bromley, 'The French Privateering War' in Ed. Bell and Ollard, *Historical Essays, 1600–1750* (1963).
A. Browning, *Thomas Osborne, Earl of Danby* (3 Volumes, 1944–51).
A. Bryant, *King Charles II* (1955).
W. S. Churchill, *Marlborough* (1933).
D. Coombs, *The Conduct of the Dutch* (The Hague, 1958).
R. Davis, 'English Foreign Trade, 1660–1700', *Economic History Review*, 2nd Series, VII, 2 (1954).
J. Ehrman, *The Navy in the War of William III* (1953).
K. Feiling, *British Foreign Policy, 1660–1672* (1930).
R. H. George, 'The Financial Relations of Louis XIV and James II', *Journal of Modern History*, III, 3 (1931).
C. L. Grose, '*Louis XIV's Financial Relations with Charles II*', *ibid.*, I, 2 (1929).
C. H. Hartmann, *Charles II and Madame* (1934).
    Clifford of the Cabal (1937).

J. P. Kenyon, *Robert Spencer, Earl of Sunderland* (1958).

M. Priestley, 'Anglo-French Trade and the "Unfavourable Balance" Controversy', *Economic History Review*, 2nd series, IV (1951–52).

M. A. Thomson, 'Louis XIV and the Origins of the War of the Spanish Succession', *Transactions of the Royal Historical Society*, 5th series, IV (1954).

   'Louis XIV and the Grand Alliance', *Bulletin of the Institute of Historical Research*, XXXIV (1961).

Documents

H. Davis (Ed.), J. Swift, *Political Tracts, 1711–1713* (1964).

G. M. Trevelyan, *Select Documents for Queen Anne's Reign* (1929).

Chapter 8

R. Colie, *Light and Enlightenment* (1957).

P. Hazard, *The European Mind, 1680–1715* (1964).

R. S. Westfall, *Science and Religion in Seventeenth-Century England* (New Haven, 1958).

Time Chart

———

1604   Peace with Spain.

1609   Twelve Years Truce between Dutch and Spain.

1613   Elizabeth married to Frederick.
Sarmiento (Gondomar) Ambassador.

1614   Cokayne project.
Addled Parliament.

1616   Transfer of cautionary towns to Dutch.

1617   Raleigh's Orinocco voyage.
Spanish marriage negotiations announced.

1618   Bohemian rising.

1619   Frederick accepts Bohemian throne.
Synod of Dort.

1620   White Mountain, Bohemians defeated.

1621   Resumption of Dutch–Spanish war.
Vere in the Palatinate.
James clashes with Parliament over foreign policy.

1622   Palatinate overrun.

1623   March–October, Charles in Madrid.
Massacre of Amboyna.

1625   Congress at The Hague.
Cadiz expedition.
French marriage.

1627   Ile de Ré expedition.

1628   Assassination of Buckingham.
Fall of La Rochelle.

1629   Dissolution of Parliament.
Peace with France.

1630   Peace with Spain.

1634   First Writ of Ship Money.

1639   Tromp attacks Spanish fleet in Downs.
First Bishops' War.

1640   Second Bishops' War.

1641   Marriage of William and Mary.
Irish rising.

1648 Treaties of Münster (peace between Spain and Dutch) and Westphalia.

1649 End of the first Fronde.
Murder of Dorislaus.
Danes give Dutch preferential tolls.
Cromwell in Ireland.

1650 Second Fronde.
September, Battle of Dunbar.
December, Spanish recognition.

1651 Navigation Ordinance.
Battle of Worcester.

1652 May, Surrender of Galway. Clash off Dover with Tromp.
Summer, Blake and Tromp in Northern waters.
August, De Ruyter in Channel.
September, Kentish Knock.
November, Tromp outward bound, Dungeness.

1653 February, Tromp inward bound, Portland.
April, expulsion of Rump.
June, Gabbard. Close blockade.
July, Terheide
October, Fall of Bordeaux.

1654 April, Peace of Westminster.
Commercial Treaty with Portugal.

1655 April, Attempt on San Domingo.
October, War with Spain.

1657 Anglo-French alliance.

1658 Battle of the Dunes, Dunkirk taken.

1659 Fleet sent to the Sound.
Treaty of the Pyrenees.

1660 Peace with Spain.
Navigation Act.

1661 Danish treaty on Sound tolls.

1662 Dunkirk sold.
September, Dutch treaty.

1663 Staple act.

1664 De Ruyter in West Africa.
New York taken.
Colbert's first tariff.
December, Allin attacks Smyrna convoy.

1665 March, War with Dutch.
May, Lowestoft.
July–August, Sandwich off Norway, Bergen.

1666 War with France and Denmark.
June, Four Days' Fight.
July, North Foreland.

1667 May, French invade Spanish Netherlands.
June, Dutch attack Chatham.
July, Treaty of Breda.
Heavy French tariffs.
Commercial treaty with Spain.

1668 Franco-Austrian secret partition treaty.
Triple Alliance.
Treaty of Aachen.

1670 Secret Treaty of Dover.

1671 Simulated Treaty.

1672 April, Attack on Smyrna convoy. War.
June, Solebay.
August, De Witts lynched.

1673 June, Schooneveld.
August, Kijkduin.
James marries Mary of Modena.
Test Act.

1674 Peace with Dutch.

1677 French take Cambrai and Valenciennes.
Marriage of William and Mary.

1678 Troops sent to Ostend.
Treaty of Nijmegen.
October, Popish Plot.

1679 Exclusion bill introduced.

1680 Spanish treaty.

1681 French subsidies to Charles.
Oxford Parliament dissolved.
French occupy Strasbourg.

1683 Relief of Vienna.

1684 Louis takes Luxemburg.
Truce of Ratisbon.

1685 Revocation of Edict of Nantes.

1686 League of Augsburg.

1688 September, Beginning of European war.
November, William lands at Torbay.

1689 Bantry Bay.
Siege of Derry.

1690 June, Beachy Head.
The Boyne.
Fleurus.

1691 Surrender of Limerick.

1692 May, Barfleur–La Hougue.
Namur lost.
Steenkirk.

1693   Smyrna fleet attacked off Portugal.
       Landen.

1694   Attempt against Brest.

1695   Namur retaken.

1697   Treaty of Ryswick.
       Visit of Peter the Great.

1698   First Partition Treaty.
       Scots settle Darien.

1700   March, Second Partition Treaty.
       October, Will of Carlos II.
       November, His death. Accession of Philip V.
       Start of Great Northern War.

1701   Grand Alliance of the Hague.
       Louis recognizes James III.

1702   March, Death of William III.
       May, allies declare war.

1703   Methuen Treaty with Portugal.

1704   Capture of Gibraltar, battle of Malaga.
       Blenheim.
       Scottish Act of Security.

1705   Capture of Barcelona.

1706   Ramillies. Flanders conquered.
       French defeated at Turin.

1707   Unsuccessful attack on Toulon.
       Italian neutrality treaty.
       Almanza.
       Union treaty with Scotland.

1708   Oudenarde, Wynendael.
       Lille captured.
       French expedition against Scotland.

1709   Swedes defeated at Poltava.
       First Barrier Treaty.
       September, Malplaquet.

1710   Brihuega.
       Douai and Aire taken.
       Gertruydenberg negotiations.
       August, Godolphin dismissed.

1711   Bouchain taken.
       Archduke Charles elected emperor.
       October, preliminaries agreed with France.

1712   Dismissal of Marlborough.
       Utrecht Conference began.
       Allies defeated at Denain.

1713   Treaties of Utrecht.
       Rejection of commercial clauses.

Index